INTRODUCTION

I never thought I would sit down and start writing a book. Especially one about me or have anything interesting enough in my life to do so. That changed. Well, maybe I did when crazy shit happened or I told someone about it, then of course, they would suggest with the typical line, "Dude, you should write a book man, that shit is crazy!", or "You missed your calling." I never thought I would see the day that I'm actually doing, and It is because of the incentive of family that got me here, new love, life and very good friends, mentors, and let's be honest, maybe some psychiatrists too, that I am writing this. I consider it a huge 'rant' if you will, but here it goes.

Let me first explain the title:

By no means am I claiming my life or name to be of the religious term "Divine". It is simply my name, and "Intervention" has always been my call sign overseas during missions to protect my identity. Mostly because I have had a long-life habit of intervening and stopping shit, my business or not. The rest, well I will let the reader decide or find out what he or she takes from it. Is it because of surviving and living after attacks near fatal? Having confrontations, ins and outs with careers, and relationships? you decide your own take on it as I said.

"Everything is Kung Fu! "Kung Fu lives in everything we do. It lives in how we put on the jacket, how we take off the jacket. It lives in how we treat people! Everything is Kung Fu" (2010 Karate Kid remake -Jackie Chan)

This book is by no means an instructional, Martial arts how to book, or anything to do with fighting although some mentioned. Kung Fu in its own true definition is just Time spent in a skillset, an endeavor or hard work. There is no totality, just like in life. This quote from Jackie Chan's character in that remade version of 'Karate Kid' should have been called "Kung Fu Kid," since it was that skill set, mindset, setting that was displayed. But that is my take on it. If I wanted this book to be about the art, or practical, it would be called Wu Shu, which is by definition "War art. "

The "Kung Fu" part in my life, although some semi-fictionalized parts in this autobiography, is what one person, on Quora wrote, that perfectly defines Jackie Chan's quote as:

"Not being about fighting. It is about bettering yourself. This must reflect on your life, in every action. It's about being Honest, Kind, and compassionate. It's about fairness, leadership and confidence.

I will paraphrase the rest by saying

"To be a Martial Artist, or to be able to call yourself one, every action should reflect the best version of yourself. Every action that you do should show the people around you that you are a Martial Artist, not just a mindless fighter" This is the meaning of "Everything is Kung Fu"

My philosophy is a combination of all these attributes, but as you will see in my story, it's about how it all comes back to us. Our decisions, our reactions and interactions and how we stimulate, respond, influence, emulate or reject their affect. There are many lessons I have learned, some over and over and I would, if given the chance, go back and change or do better with. That's why it's called life. You only get one.

If you're the kind of person that cannot handle very blunt unpolitically correct or hard-core talk about life, then close the book right now and get your money back if It publishes one day. As I said above, I never thought about writing a book about me and I don't believe myself to be the kind to use the proper etiquette it takes to be considered a great writer or that I deserve to be in the same category as them. With that in mind, if you decide to read on, then I thank you for your patience. My goal in writing this book is to hopefully give some comfort to those who have been through most or all that I have been through, you are not alone. Some of you, no, in fact a lot of you, have probably thought about writing your own stories, but had no time, were too lazy or busy feeling sorry for yourself in a bar or in your bed pillow drowning in your own pit of BS, or were afraid of losing your job, or just have no balls to say the things I have to. See? Did that hurt your feelings? For those of you who are not veterans of the Military, or Law Enforcement like I am, we have a saying, and it goes like this. "A fairy tale starts with "Once upon a time" a real story told by someone like me, although again some parts are semi fictionalized for identity purposes, content of actions or other reasons, and starts with "This is no shit!" well, "This is no shit" so enjoy!

ACKNOWLEDGEMENT

First and foremost I want to thank my wife Zuka who has encouraged me to wipe the dust off some projects I have put away in pursuing like this as well as other efforts I gave up on but with her patience and push, I have succeeded in so much. To my sons Michael, Brandon and Ryan, I wish I was around more in your life to pass on my teachings earlier and more often, and I thank God every day I still have you in my life. My late father, who I know only wanted to assure me that I would be a better man and straight on my path. My late mother who was always there to come to and keep me focused on my emotional health as well as physical. My late uncle Pat, who was a great Judo expert that I did not know until later in my life, but still got to learn some good lessons from and stories. Of course, a special thanks to all relatives, for your patience and support of me during the years together and apart.

In this story, I will be mentioning friends, groups and mentors like my great Martial Arts Master and Mentor, Master Wong of the Master Wong System, to which I am now a proud certified instructor under and opening a better version of myself by not only guiding my physical and technique development but digging deep and pushing me to "express myself" as Bruce Lee had been quoted. Master Wong wants us to face and bring out all that has made us who we are today. The Demons, the Hard times, the good times, struggles, awarding, all of it. They gave me the inspiration to inspire others with some of my life experiences and surviving some deadly ones. I also want to thank Tony Schiena, who I got to train many forces with overseas, and allowed me to assist in many instructional DVDs and showed up to offer critical guidance when needed in many Danger Zones. I cannot thank TBBG (The Black Belt Gathering) group Founders Ed Hartzell, Billy Eggert enough, and other great names and members included for nominating and accepting me as a Sage Council member and letting me be a part of a Martial Arts Family again to participate and contribute to. If I've left out any other names of family and friends who have inspired me in my life, then I apologize but you know who you are, and it is for good reason. I do not need certain people in my life past and present to know who or where you are. I have hurt many or at least inconvenienced them or their lives in some way, and I am sure if given the chance they would do the same to you if not to me. As I said, I consider this a huge rant, so if some stories, some time frames, or any detail seems confusingly jumpy, it's because I'm just thinking out loud as it comes to me, but I have no apologies, so sorry if it sounds like a living will, but tough shit. In this book, although based on true events, some scenarios, actions taken, names of people, places, and details were left out, or could be changed to avoid any fallout of feelings, job security, and overall lives, or their wellbeing, compromised.

Chapter One

"THE DEERWOOD DRAGON"

OK here we go. Let's get all the usual beginnings out of the way. First, just like most of my brothers, I go by the shortcut version of my name Terrence, so call me Terry, only my mother called me Terrence. I was born and raised in the suburbs of New York. Lived in Rockland County for most of my life on Deerwood Drive in New City. I am second to youngest in a family of five boys and one girl. The oldest Brother "Matthew" is now deceased and same with my dad (Matt Sr.) both passing in the same year 2002, but I will not get into that too much or at all and let them rest in peace. What is amazing about my memory is that I can remember most if not all my childhood but cannot remember the few past years all in detail. I had an OK childhood, not a great one, but an OK one I can honestly say. We were raised fair but very hard and from what I hear from my siblings during my younger years some of us were raised harder than others. I am not one that will ever claim to be an angel. I was never one, then or now. I was just as thick headed, and stubborn as I am now. Typical NY Irish catholic family upbringing. Sometimes that worked for me, but most of the time, it got me in trouble. I'm not going to spend a lot of time talking about my younger childhood days, but I will highlight some of the good, the funny, the bad times and the base that made me who I am today, or something like that, so, you're welcome!

I was trouble from the start. I was told that as soon as I could understand words. I found out that if my father did not bring my mother to the hospital the day I was born, that she and I would have died together because it took forever to come out and she almost bled to death. She was passing it off as bad cramps or gas and refused to go to the hospital for a while until my dad insisted. I can say a few funny but true things about my childhood, like the way I thought and behaved was 90% from TV. Just like most kids I believed in superheroes, I believed in good vs. evil and winning, and that everybody could do those things, but I wanted to be the one to save the day. I always looked up to my older brothers and my one sister, and especially today my younger brother. Their wit, humor and their strength, as well as their popularity always inspired me to be and learn more. I would sneak out of my bedroom whenever I heard the older ones have guests. I could overhear the music, and TV shows, and even some records with adult theme humor. I would also wear their clothes to elementary school that had nightclub names on it and we're obviously 'Adult' in theme. Getting back to superheroes, my favorites were the usual like most. Superman, Spiderman, Batman...(Still is) and the bionic man which was also called "The six million dollar man" on the TV series followed by the Hulk. My grandmother on my mother's side would make us knitted webs for Spiderman play, and capes for Superman or Batman Play. In those days I honestly believed I could be the one to save the day, not get hurt, and if I was lucky, get the girl at the end. It took me a long time, even all the way up to and through high school to realize that... I could not..., and that I was not invincible. One of my brothers, the second oldest, Patrick, was into martial arts, Tae Kwon Do, so to complement my superhero thinking as a child, I of course wanted to study too but was turned down for a while by my parents. To compensate, I would imitate my brother, and I would watch the movies on TV like Kung Fu theatre, The Chinese English dubbed over ones and then go practice those moves in a bathrobe I pretended was a Karate uniform, not knowing what the fuck I was doing but it looked good. I would break panel boards and do flying kicks and imitate all the animal styles I saw with sound effects of course. My parents thought it was a phase I was going through and were against me learning because I was not mature enough to understand the balance between real life, responsibility, and the art, but still let me learn hoping it would discipline me, because I had a temper. It took me years to be as good as my older brother who had a natural talent and was always better than his rank, even when I surpassed him later. Just like in some movies or TV shows, I had to face a few bullies who wanted to test how much I knew. Back then, there was still a martial arts code to only use martial arts for self-defense. That rule now only exists in movies from what I see. My father also warned me never to fight in school or get in trouble. One bully stands out and he knows who he is. His name was John. Yes, I know..., just like "Johnny from Karate Kid". He picked on me verbally with his friends, never alone, since "Pop Warner football" (Peewee, Midget, Jr. Midget,) etc... All the way to high school. Like I said, I never fought because of words. You can call me pussy, a wimp, and call my mother anything you wanted, and I still would not fight for just words. I will get back to that bully later. When I started in martial arts as a child, at first it was because of those movies I was very attracted to like the Bruce Lee ones, then the flashy Kung Fu forever fights, and eventually the competitive Kickboxing occasionally I saw in the ring with belts tied around silky kickbox pants. To show myself and others what I could do when I put my mind to it, I would always dress the part and demonstrate anything I watched. My determination to learn as much as possible came about when one day I was walking with my younger brother, cutting through our elementary school up the street from our family's house, that we came across some punks we knew, and they were tripping some kid, planting him on his ass, laughing and doing it again. So, of course I said something, got taken down, got up and challenged them again and again to show I could take it. My younger brother opened his mouth and one of the punks started wailing on him, but my brother covered up pretty well. While making our way home, I vowed to my younger brother that I would be a Master, and it would never ever happen again! I mean, the only hitting we were used to was not just getting disciplined, but we played stupidly dangerous games like turning off the lights and smack fighting if we could find each other or hide and go seek (Then Kill the guy) in the dark by tackling the guy you find. We would trip and thought it was cool seeing blue flashes when we smacked our heads on furniture when we tripped or got taken down in the living room. Sick, but true. We, meaning my younger brother Greg and I, would also lay on the couch and play the game of Up Down Push, which is when you both lay down, straight lined where only your feet meet in the middle. With equal force you would keep your feet against each other, raise your legs slightly tucked (Up) then lower them back to the middle (Down) then as hard as we can on the (Push), we would try to overpower and push one another off the couch with just your feet. 99% of the time, it turned into a heel smashing kick fight.

Back to my Mastering vow…Later after a while of learning whatever and wherever I could, it got to the point that I cut school to go to competitions or to learn somewhere secretly, when my parents pulled me out as punishment for letting it interfere with my academics. I remember one time I cut school with a friend of mine to go to New York City for competition and another time to Chinatown to shop for cool Martial Arts stuff. I thought I could make it home before my parents did from work, well at least my dad. My mom would think I was just coming home from school, but I was not so lucky. One time, although I took first place at a tournament I was forbidden to go to, I lost the match with my mom when I got home. I did not cover my bases and the school called looking for me. My mom was the real ninja that day by throwing silverware from the kitchen accurately at my head when I lied about where I was. I do believe that one of the pieces of silverware stuck into the wall like a cartoon making that vibrating noise. It didn't matter how big the trophy was, my father was bigger and had his turn when he came home. Now that I think about it, I was stupid at my young age to be taking a bus to New York City and try to get back all within 8 hours to fool my parents. Ok…getting ahead of myself, Like I said, timeframes will jump. I go on tangents.

In elementary school I had a few scuffles but nothing major or more than the average kid fights. It was mostly the usual who called who what. It would be the hair pulling, tripping, wild swinging, nobody won type that was always broken up. What I'm telling you next is no shit too. In fourth grade or so, my parents decided to let me try going to catholic school, a big mistake. I hated the uniform, I hated the nuns, I hated the ugly ass principal, who looked like John Denver and Elton John had a daughter. I hated all of them. My fourth-grade teacher, a nun, that I called "Sister fat Bitch," (Looked Like fat Elvis version) had a rule about touching things on her desk.

One day, I was holding pamphlets, like a comic book version of biblical stories, to put on desks for her. As I walked by her desk, the sharp wing tip of this big ass Eagle, that was welded on a copy of the Liberty Bell she used to ring for recess got caught on my sleeve, scraped me, made me bleed and dropped to the floor making the ringing sound. As if it was not bad enough, and remember... I am hurt, all the kids jumped up thinking it was time to go outside. They saw me holding my arm and the bell on the floor and started laughing. Before I could say a word or recover, I felt a choking hand from behind squeezing my neck and WHAM!! WHAM! Right across my head and face back and forth. "Sister Fat Fuck", hit me with no mercy. I turned around so fast with a scream and a punch to her stomach, I swear, I could have broken a stack of 10 boards with that punch. She went flying and lost her breath. I thought I was done for and turned green and sick to my stomach from it all. When she recovered, she took me by my hand, sat me at my desk and told me to look at the cross and pray to Jesus, while the other kids played outside. With huge tears in my eyes, snot from my nose onto the hard desk, and shaky crying words I prayed to Jesus to kill her and told him I hated her. My mom picked me up and when I told her what happened, she told me the same kind of shit happened to her and that her mother came for her and threatened the nun like my mom did that day for me when she realized Sister "Fat Elvis `` hit me. Needless to say, I hated it so much I refused to do any work for the rest of the year and got left back in fourth grade and switched back to public school, heh heh, heh, all part of a master plan.

I was not really that well behaved back at public school either. I remember one time; teachers were on strike and blocked us from walking into school and said, "go home" and shit like that. One even grabbed my arm when I tried going around them. Big mistake, because the next day, I brought my father's Blackjack (Mini Spring Club with steel tip) wound in leather and hid it in my back pocket, "Just in case". Well, no issues outside or getting into school, but during art class, my teacher, or substitute that day lifted it right out of my pocket while walking by my desk while she was reading some bullshit. I told her to give it back and she cannot go into my pocket and take my stuff. The principal, Mr. Del V, had a different opinion and told me he doesn't care what kind of excuse, or Bullshit I studied like Karate, and all that, and that my father would have to come and get it. I waited a few days and hoped my father would not get a call, he didn't. But…he did ask my mother out loud, and intentionally in front of us all, "Where is my black jack.?" Out of 6 kids in my family, he immediately turned to me and asked if I knew where it was. I asked "What the hell is a blackjack? He told me after telling me to watch my mouth, by describing it like I did earlier. I said "nope", "the only thing I had like that was my foam Nunchakus." with a nervous laugh

After that interrogation from my dad, I knew I had to do something. The school had given a day off to attend some meetings regarding the teachers but held somewhere else, so I knew nobody would be at my school except the janitor, maybe, Mr. Luth. I went there by foot as always because it was literally up the street from where my house was through a tiny woods section. I went full ninja mask sneaking around until I saw if he was there or not. He was sweeping the cafeteria. I took off the Ninja shit and went up to the doors and knocked after hiding my costume I had over my regular clothes. I asked Mr. Luth to please let me quickly run in and go to my desk that we had cubby holes in because I left workbooks and stuff my parents wanted me to do during break and I would get in trouble. He knew our family well since we all milled through there at some point from oldest to youngest. I ran straight to the principal's office, opened every drawer and cabinet, and there was my father's blackjack handle, sticking out from under some memo pads. I grabbed that shit along with some pads and ran around the back to another hall to make it look like I was coming from my classroom and thanked Mr. Luth for "Saving my butt". I snuck that blackjack back under my dad's t-shirts in one of his drawers. Mission Impossible Completed. "Sorry dad."

I already had a growth spurt before or at sixth grade and still had that superhero complex I talked about earlier, so of course I would brag to my friends then about how much I could lift or bench in my downstairs laundry room gym. One day, when they wanted to see how much I could lift, or just to use the weights themselves, they came over to my house. I lived only minutes from our public elementary school. I always went through the garage into the basement directly, well, most of the time anyway to avoid dealing with my mom or anyone right away. I let everybody in and offered to get them some peanut butter on toast and orange juice mixed with milk, which was my super food for lifting back then. I went upstairs and thought I heard one of my brothers in the living room with the TV on. I did not bother looking and went directly into the kitchen. After a few lifts, one of the other kids wanted some of the same snack, so I went back upstairs but the TV was off. I slowly poked my head around the corner of the doorway leading to the staircase to look inside the living room and noticed a stranger, a full-grown man, shuffling through some shelves near the couch. Without taking one step, I jumped down those stairs and told the kids that I had a stranger in my house robbing us and to get out through the basement door. Making our escape one of the kids tripped on some frozen mud and looked up and the man inside was staring right at him, he tearfully yelled and pointed at the window. By the time we looked up we could see the shadow of the guy moving through the house to maybe come after us we thought. We all ran next door to my neighbors at the time and told them about the stranger in my house and they called the police. Minutes later, my second oldest brother Patrick, I mentioned earlier, the other karate guy, drove up. I yelled to him not to go into the house and said there was a robber. He quickly whipped out the biggest cool Chinese star I have ever seen and went in after ripping his jacket off. I swear I thought I was going to see a man fly out the window. My brother came out with a shrug saying he found no one. The police arrived finally and did their own search and felt that the guy came out the basement like us and went through the backyard to escape while we were reporting it. I was so proud of my brother, and he still is an idol to me. They all are in their own way. The same brother I remember threw this neighborhood bully "Kevin" down the hill on the top of our block when I failed to defend my younger brother from him. The kid whipped my legs with a BB rifle gun of some sort. All I remember is that it was ice cold outside, and it hurt. I think my sister slapped him around too...lol. My sister also kicked the shit out of a girl her age that I thought liked me. I told my sister I caught the girl and her friends smoking weed in my local woods up the street we cut across to go to the store, and she offered me to try it while laughing. That was too cool to see my sister slap the shit out of someone. She still is very strong minded and blunt. She never gave herself enough credit about how beautiful of a person she was and still is. I called her Mommy #2. For the good reasons of being there to talk to when I needed to, but also the bad times she would act as a second voice of my mother echoing the same lectures or telling on me when I did something wrong. I deserved it.

My superhero complex did not humble me even after that event at the house when I ran almost crying in fear. Especially when it came time I discovered "girls" and believed I was Sir Galahad, white knight in shining armor for all the damsels in distress. If any boy hurt their feelings, teased them, or made them cry, the music in my head would start! Da da da daaaaa, there I was to confront them with my one eyebrow up and manly voice with a karate pose warning that I will defend them and to back off. That syndrome lasted and worked for the girls for a while until I got educated the hard way later in life, in the art of their manipulation. The lies told and stories just to see the one that hurt their feelings "get theirs." I cannot count on my hands alone how many guys I have "Taught a lesson" to in my life because of some BS some little trick told me as the truth. Everything from "he did this to me" and "he used me" and even as serious and false accusations of rape in later years when all he did was find another girlfriend after he had her or she was just a Ho and would know I would find out she gave it up to a few at once so tried to play victim. At one point when I was still "Going after the evil doers" One guy begged me for his life and told me the real deal between him and this one girl who cried her story to me about false accusations of abuse, rape and even getting her pregnant and leaving. When I confronted the girl, she admitted that it was all BS and said she was just pissed for him breaking up with her after they had a "relationship" which turned out to be just a sexual one. I mean, I left this guy just breathing thinking he really did this all to her, so that's when I decided to just step back and open my eyes to the evil that people do. I say I've learned my lesson but later in the years I guess I forgot and started trusting people again and fell for the same tricks and BS even during and after High school. I will discuss examples later.

On my block and nearby (Deerwood Dr) you would have the typical games played amongst the neighbor's kids that I became friends with like, hide and go seek, ring Alivio, kickball, baseball red light green light etc. But of course, I had to cater to my own ego and have my own little gang that I called the 'Deerwood Dragons' and teach whatever I could to the neighborhood kids most of which were younger than me or at least the same age. I called it a gang, but we really did nothing. I would give them little dragon patches or stickers, I would get from a flea market here and there, or some Martial Art looking things like a Yin

Yang symbol or anything I thought was cool. We really had fun, set a routine of hangout time, dinner time call of parents whistling or yelling for us to come home you can hear all over the neighborhood. I would have a girlfriend that was of course by title only "Going Out" but would consist of nothing but walking together, showing off for, and holding a hand maybe, but anything else was too awkward and too shy at that early age to try. If I did, it was met with a push and warning that her parents might see, even from 1/4 mile away. I was a perv..lol.

Besides martial arts I had the usual childhood side interests like cub scouts, and like I said I tried each kind of sport mostly to make my father happy like Little League baseball after T shirt league or what we used to call pee wee type football which I had no clue (like I said) of what I was doing. I know I drove my father crazy with my lack of knowledge of what was going on the football field, like how many players there are, or their positions, or what my job was as a defensive tackle or wherever they placed my little butt. One memory I do have is when we traveled to Massachusetts to play the opposite team and families would take in the visiting players. The kid I stayed with decided to play a joke with his friends while I was sleeping and take a sharpie permanent marker to my face, having me wake up and look in the mirror seeing full black lines and a few choice words on my face. I got my revenge, because I told them I was going to sleep a little longer while they went to church or something, and they all went out of the house. I went exploring and stole about $80 worth of coins that they had hidden in a big tube container in their closet. Hoping they would blame him. Victory was mine! LOL. Cub Scouts was no picnic either, because my den father, well, to tell you the truth, his whole family was very weird, and I'm convinced there were a lot of role playing games going on in that family. I say this because it's the truth. There was one point where we stayed over at our troop den father's house. His son that I went to elementary school with, at least Catholic school, had his own superhero. It was Wonder Woman. In the middle of the night while sleeping over I felt his arm lock in with mine and when I woke up, I asked him what he's doing. He asked if he could sleep naked next to me. I told him to go to the other side of the room into his own bed and after arguing back and forth I turned on the light and lo and behold he had a full Wonder Woman outfit on with tin foil eagle on the chest, blue spandex shorts, red tube top, the works! I couldn't sleep the rest of the night. I told him to stay on the other side of the room in his own bed. I think I told very few people to this day. The next morning at breakfast I took a very close look at this sister and at the mother and then directly in the eyes of his father. I have nothing against anyone's sexual preferences, but do not force it on me. All I can say is sometimes when you look at people you could tell their parents were brother and sister, and in the words of the great Forrest Gump character "That's all I have to say about that."

My room at home was always decorated with whatever I was interested in or whoever my current idol was. I had the usual black light, velvet colorful posters. Everything from Bruce Lee to Elvis Presley. I would always wear theme type clothes with whatever I was imitating that day. It would be" Rocky" one day or"Elvis `` or"Bruce Lee." I always was the oddball, the black sheep of the family and I still am. I lived for watching TV anytime with a big bowl of cereal in my lap and could watch all in a row nightly. I knew what was going to be on what night. Favorites were in a row some nights, like Odd Couple, Fantasy Island, Love Boat, Captain and Tennille, Donny and Marie, Sonny and Cher, All in the Family, Good Times, Jeffersons, Sanford and Son, Happy days etc. I had a childhood friend who acted like the Fonz' from 'Happy Days'. We thought it was cool. Zumbo was his last name. Jeans, White T-shirt, slick back the black hair or greased back with a comb from the pocket and snap his fingers or thumbs up with an "AAAAYYYYY", or a thumbs down telling you to "Sit on it," or "You're a Nerd"

On weekends if not after school sometimes, it was Looney

Tunes, Kroft Superstars, Land of the lost, Hong Kong Phooey (Of Course) and a series of different characters like Batman and Robin (70s version), Shazam!, Dr. Shrinker, HR Puffin stuff or whatever, Sigmund the Sea Monster, and on Sundays after church and breakfast it was the lineup of Abbot and , Chiller theater, or the Kung Fu Movies, if not the Superheroes I mentioned earlier including Lone Ranger episodes. We all imitated our favorites. From Elvis, to the Fonz' to Miami Vice fashion in later years. I remember and see reruns available now on cable of situation comedy or life lesson ones like Partridge family, Brady Bunch, Family Affair, Different Strokes, Facts of Life, etc. It's funny to see how cheesy they are now as an adult but so riveting as a child.

Now back to the bullies. In junior high I decided to run an intramural self-defense club for a class of kids with special needs with the guidance of a teacher "Mr. G", who was very popular with the kids and a great man all around. Once it was revealed that I knew any kind of martial arts, it opened a whole shark tank of ass holes who wanted to test me. I heard of this one huge black kid "Richard" before I even got to junior high. I heard about how huge his arms were, how many kids he beat up, and that all his family had the same reputation, sisters included. I must admit the way the kids in my neighborhood described him, I was scared. I was so nervous but curious about this kid. When I started Jr. High, and got to homeroom, I asked randomly, to who I was sitting next to about him by name. This kid just looked at me with his eyebrows up in a cautious and curious look and told me he was Richard, and what about him.?. I looked at him from head to toe, and he was not as big or mean or scary as all the stories I heard. I reached out my hand to shake his while I introduced myself. We got along, for a little while anyway until of course some assholes decided to see the huge black kid Vs. the Karate kid by making up and spreading rumors that I called him the "N" word, and that I could take him. As soon as I heard this rumor as kind of a warning to me that he was looking for me, I sought him out and cleared the air. It did take a lot of calming down to listen over the crowd of kids encouraging a fight, like straight out of a movie, but I did convince him that it was all bullshit. I could tell though, that he was curious and maybe even anxious to also see who would win. Even though we were cool that day with each other, their friendship was not the same, in fact, he started playing pranks and living up to his reputation that included me with some physical abuse at my locker by thrusting his knee into my leg. It did not have the effect that he expected like the other kids that went down, so he would try it again two or three more times and still with no effect, so he gave up. I probably could have and should have defended myself back then but like I said we were kind of friends, and I took it as a prank not a threat. There was one huge fat kid taller than most teachers who I caught one day throwing smaller kids against lockers for fun. I of course being a superhero and Sir Galahad approached him and told to stop. He towered over me at least by a foot and said I was known as a wimp in this school and to fuck off. I personally thought I had a great reputation in the school, and I am far from being a wimp and let him know that. He reached his hands out to grab me, so I turned sideways and smacked him in the balls with the back of my hand putting him down instantly and even made his man boobs shake. I really, ... at least still at this point, did not have a mean or violent streak in me, not yet anyway, otherwise I would have finished him off with a knee to his face. I don't remember really what happened after that, if I ran or got a teacher, or ever saw him again. I must admit I liked the attention I got from being known as a karate instructor, but it still brought the wrong kind of attention from some. Another popular kid "Steve" was a really decent looking lady's man type who seemed he could get any girl he wanted at such a young age, but he had the most popular beautiful girl in school as his girlfriend. Even though he was a pretty boy, I would see him during study hall having slap fights outside with the black kid I described earlier. I was kind of curious and jealous of this kid and his popularity, but I was more impressed with his slap fights and relationship with the other kid. As the year went by, I guess the students got bored and decided to spread another rumor that I was talking shit about this pretty boy. I think it was the Jr. High prom night, I went to the bathroom to splash my face when suddenly, the walls filled with kids like they were waiting for a movie to start. I was so confused that I myself went to one of the sinks against the wall and sat down wondering what was going on and what I was waiting to see. Just as I sat down looking towards the door in walks in Mr. Popular. He was walking in a ninja stealth way, one foot crossing over the other very slowly creeping towards me with his hands up and opened. I ask them what the fuck is going on? Nobody answered. I told the kid to stop approaching me and asked if he really wants to fight now? and why? Still no answer. I got up, put my hands up as if to say stop and he tried to tackle me. When he grabbed my legs I reached down to my arm around his throat, lifted and went to the floor holding him there and told him to stop and that there was no reason to continue. Some kids doing lookout I guess yelled inside the bathroom that the teachers were coming. I let him up and quickly went to the wall to look like we were hanging out talking. I had broken blood vessels in his eyes by choking him in the headlock and they looked like red bloody chips in his eyes that I could see while he was looking in the mirror and fixing himself. When one or two teachers came in and ask what's going on? I told them we're hanging out and bored with the prom. I could tell they expected to see a fight, but we quickly stopped in time. They threw us out of the bathroom and told us to go back to the hall where the dancing was. I cannot say this guy was a bully, but just another misinformed one that fell for the bullshit that others will make up for their own entertainment. He shook my hand and said he did not want any problems and that we were cool, and had a good fight and other cheese dick stuff. I knew I could have beaten him, but glad I did not because he ended up being a cool friend, well somewhat of one after that night.

Chapter Two
"LEARNING 'The Way' THE HARD WAY"

When I was a young kid, starting out in Martial arts I was never satisfied with my rank and actually lied about it in the beginning to my dad who was paying for it but he would sometimes mention not seeing my belt change for months at a time and growing inpatient. When I was a white belt, I would put on stripes every few weeks to appease my dad trying to fake progression, and then remove stripes before class. Same as a greenbelt, all the way until I was a brown belt and so forth until I made at least Jr. black belt in those disciplines. I remember one time, for Halloween, I did not want to wear my green belt, so I spray painted my brother's yellow belt black, since he quit Tae Kwon Do. That did not go over so well because it dried and chipped and rubbed all over my white uniform during my go rounds for candy and looked ridiculous. I studied Goju Ryu, and Tae Kwon Do then and it took a longer time to make rank, than I see it does now with these 'McDojos' giving out Black Belts practically 2 years later. I was great at posing, doing all the air shots and forms and flashy moves but never knew what it felt like to hit someone for real or be hit except by my father of course. Like I said before my size and skills grew fast so there was not much hitting at home anymore, and I would never claim to have been abused by my parents or take advantage of my size or abuse them. I got disciplined no more than I deserved or more than any kid at my age had gone through. I found this to really be true when I was playing my younger brother in some old video game downstairs in our house and I lost or could not figure out something, and I threw down the controller. My younger brother told me to calm down and try again and I yelled "NO! I hate this Fucking game." Immediately after that loud cursing, I could hear my father's quick heavy footsteps toward the stairway door from the Living room and the fast swing of it flying open with the horrifying yell of my full name" Terrence Michael Devine get up here!". There is nothing more scary and sick feeling than your father waiting on the top of a stairway that you now have to climb in shame wondering when and where you're going to get hit. I surprisingly made it to the top and out of the staircase into the hall without a single hit. My dad looked at me head to toe and just said "so? You are a big man now, big karate and a big cursing man now?" then looked me over again. I kind of gave him a cocky look with a smirk when I realized that he noticed how tall and broad I was, like him, so he caught that and said after "don't ever think you can take me on and that you will ever be too big for a smack, I am still your father" then he gave me a little smack to the shoulder and that was it. I think I lost 10 pounds of sweat and shit in those few moments, but it made me feel good after that maybe, I was growing up and earning respect. Well, nothing wrong with wishful thinking anyways.

I had two "Girlfriends" while in Jr. High, by title only and for a short period of time. One was the niece of one of the assistant Black Belt instructors at my Goju class, and she was a green belt herself. I fucked up that relationship by getting in trouble stealing money from my mom's purse and getting caught by my dad, making me miss her birthday party at a Bowling place. Told her on the phone I could not make it, and it was because I didn't have money to get her a gift. She was very disappointed, and basically cold shouldered me in school after. I saw her at the one and only High School reunion (30th). She is a very successful Doctor and I believe author. The other girl I dated, by title only, who I knew was a brown belt at Mas Oyama Karate. I just keep going for the same type, I guess. Beautiful Philippine shy and quiet. One day, I was outside, and I saw two girls who I was cool with but didn't hang with their crowd, surprisingly mouthing off to Wendy then start grabbing her. I was going to stop it but Wendy plunged a perfect sidekick into one of them, forget who, but it was a big thump sound and push off loud "ooff!" You could hear for a mile. My kickass girl came to me crying, but later she walked down the hall between classes with her head down with a few backup friends and said she didn't want to "go out" with me anymore. I think there was some pressure or prejudice talk to her from those girls about being with me. I don't know. Oh well, it was just talk and title anyway.

I made it through the rest of Jr. High without a scratch or bad reputation and was looking forward to high school. I did have a reputation for being a sort of leader who defended or was willing to defend for someone in need. But I did not filter well yet, people's "Causes" that would warrant my attention. I was expected to lead fights against other wings of the school who just talked shit about who was cooler or better etc. I would put scissors in my pocket and go meet in the middle halls to see if any dared to show and try something at supposed set times. Nothing ever came of it.

Summers back then, if not away with family, were filled with trips to the public pool, where I loved to wear my white karate pants, no shirt and train on top of the hill. It did not matter if my parents took me out of formal training because of my lack of attention to my grades and homework because by this time, most of my instructors and friends worked me out anyway wherever I could meet them. I would even show up at different schools and some other kids I met and became friends with, just to learn some basics out of the pure generosity of their instructors, letting me train with them after they heard of me and respected my background. I should have stated earlier if I have not already, that I tried to make my dad happy by attempting to like and participate in the usual sports like football, baseball and other stuff my brothers were great at and made a name for themselves with, even my younger brother. Bottom line is that I sucked at them and was only interested and daydreamed of Martial Arts, especially after facing some assholes in my youth and my whole life and career to tell you the truth.

High School was a different world. It was made up of different worlds that I categorized by name. You had the "Jocks", the "JAPS", the "Druggies", the "Ho(s)", the "Head bangers", the "Home boys" "Guidos' and Guidettes'" and the "Nerds". My world and click, I called the "Wangs." My friends and I were the Martial Artist outcasts. We all wore bodybuilding loose baggy pants tapered on the bottom with elastic waist and cuff legs, with a Chinese or Japanese logo T-shirts of some kind that was popular back then. Fringed, mesh, OP pants or Adidas with the stripes were popular too. I have a rule, never wear anything you cannot kick in. I was also buddies with some older kids that made White satin jackets that had Great Patches of Yin-Yang and Dragons on them and said "GOLDEN DRAGON KUNG FU". I never heard of it but wanted the jacket because it was cool as hell. They customized mine with a Golden Dragon on the back and my first nickname or call sign. "Snake" written in script thread in the front. I went with them to see the instructor. His name was Ron. I saw the certificate with melted wax seal on it all in Chinese. His car was filled with Inside Kung Fu Magazines front to back, but he mostly taught kids. Even at my young age I had suspicions as a Martial Artist already for a while, that he was a fraud., and magazine reading video Black Belt. But...didn't push it. He used the same basement looking area in a Church Hall type near my neighborhood that a great Goju Ryu Instructor I know and recently reunited with after over 30 years at an event named Kevin. Real Deal Legend in the art. I watched or visited. I also took some lessons from an Okinawan style of Goju Ryu instructor named Lutz who taught one of my buddies Frankie at a Veterans Hall. It was a little different than my Japanese Goju I learned in New City from many Instructors like Dave, (Marine and Police Officer back then) son of one of my father's partners. Gary, and the main Sensei, Byrne, who my mom I could tell was very impressed with because she could not stop talking about him when she saw him demonstrate a form when I had my first class. She was evaluating to see if it was good for me. I loved bouncing around training and getting to experience the different approaches. Aiki Jitsu was also available to me as a guest participant at the same place as others but different times from Instructors Roy and Miguel, who had Explosive Aiki Jitsu styles. Nothing costs that much as it does now to learn. It was not as commercialized. At my Karate studio, you would throw $20 or a little more to someone in the office once a month depending on how many days you came and that was that. My Goju Ryu school was inside the New City Judo center founded and opened by a 5th Degree Black Belt Judo master named Shumway in 1965 but closed in 1985. I found out he passed away on Veterans Day 2010. Good friend of my dad and a Navy Veteran. He would give us the Judo tip of the day sometimes after our Karate class, and to this day, I really wish I participated in both full time since they were right next door to each other, but I had my fingers in too many bowls with Tae Kwon Do, Goju Karate, and all else I was learning at the same time.

I went to the principal right away and asked if I could start a Self Defense Martial Arts Club like I did in Jr. High. He agreed to it if there was no contact and that I had a teacher present as an advisor. I broke the rules a couple of times and got caught once without the advisor present. The principal never wanted any ifs', ands' or buts' about it, rules were rules. The club and classes after school I ran were going great for the first year and even after that and brought a lot of interested students, even some from the outside of school visiting or picking up friends. The second year of running this club, we had to use the side lobby area of the school instead of the usual cafeteria where we usually would train. This made it very open for all to see, good in some ways, but it also led to the same antics from some I faced in Jr. High with students walking by, imitating us and challenging us with Bruce Lee type of fighting cries, and poses, and some walking into the class interrupting with fight stances in my face to show off for their friends. I never fought for just these antics. Now, as I mentioned in the beginning, I had a bully "John", that really stood out above all the rest. The reason he does is because he terrorized me from earlier days as a kid all the way through High school with threats and verbal abuse. He, however, never did it alone, nor did he touch me, ..yet.

Getting back to the lobby, the different parts of it had the different clicks usually separated by the sets of stairs and rails by two levels. Everybody came to hang out in the lobby during lunch or study hall. They all filed into their areas of socialites. The bully I keep describing "John", hung out with all his friends even though he wasn't much of one. Their place in the lobby was on the balcony right above our heads where we sat. I could feel their eyes looking down at us as well as down on us if that makes any sense. Occasionally we'll get the classic favorite, the spitball, crumpled tissue or paper, or actual spit dropped on us. You would never know which one did it, so there was no use confronting them. I would just tell my friends to move or go somewhere else until the end of the break period. I guess after a while, when some others saw that I would do nothing and put up with the abuse, they must have gotten the impression that I was weak or a pussy, just like the one with man boobs in junior high. I don't remember his name to this day, but there was one that called me a fag or some "gay reference", every day while walking behind me in the halls. As with the others, I never touched until I was touched. One day, this guy must have thought that I did not hear him and grabbed my shoulder hard to turn me around while saying "You hear me fag?" I turned around so fast, maybe even before he finished his question and hammer fisted him in the groin sending him backward into the lockers. I could see the shock in his eyes, that I fought back, and I kept a melting expression on my face with flaring eyes and warned him never to touch or come near me again. At least this mother fucker had the balls to follow me and touch me directly, not like one of those asshole friends of the Bully, who I was eventually cool with later named Coyle. He looked for and found my younger brother in school and tried to hurt him to get to me. I got a call from the nurse's office to come down and I also heard from a lot of kids that this ass wipe either hit my brother and or threatened him. He made a huge mistake because my younger brother was as big as me, strong as a brick house and was very popular being the football star and idol to most in school. I found this fucker after I talked to my brother who said he was ok, and I threw that fucker down the stairs. Ok a couple of stairways. I told him that if anybody wants to test me and threaten me, to come to me face to face, and don't be a chicken shit and use my family like some fucking movie. It was a quiet year after that. I still ran the Self Defense club and even had help from others skilled for variety like one Korean kid who knew Tae Kwon Do, had a uniform, and Black Belt straight from the homeland. Junior year came and I was introduced to a Man, (Mr. C) who taught an art mainly influenced by Wing Chun Kung Fu (Bruce Lee's main based theme art.) He called it 'Kuen Pai'. He agreed to come to our school and be the advisor and even teach for the club instead of a staff member who knew nothing or had their own agenda leaving me hanging sometimes to cancel. As I said before, I was not great academically so I forged all my energy into Martial Arts of all styles that I could learn, especially free ones. I still cut school or left early occasionally to compete or learn anywhere.

As I said earlier, we would get a few outsiders that were there visiting friends after school, or during class or picking them up. There were two girls that came and participated occasionally but would make open comments when I stretched, about my flexibility and my ass and how handy that would be, and the usual innuendo. I really got attracted to one of them, she went by 'Di', and she would show up in a huge brown truck outside just to catch me before going home and offer for me to go with her to different places. When I asked her why she had such a big truck, she said it was her boyfriend's and that they live together. Now, I was raised with a way that you do not take or fool around with another guy's girl, but she was addictive and made it seem ok all the time. I may have been in high school and going on Senior year, but I was still a virgin, was scared shit of getting anyone pregnant and did not know a lot except my hormones. Again, I had no experience. I mean I have kissed girls, got a BJ from and supposedly (In her words, "Got laid" from one girl I dated and fooled around with at the local pool. She will claim to this day that she was my first, but sorry honey, not the case. Don't get excited and think I am going to make this book into a teenage movie by getting into details, but I will say this, that girl was my first hard crush, not love. I was in lust with her. The first to teach me how to get over being shy about sex, especially her being a taken older woman, first to teach me how to use a condom, first to give me a "Hickey," (That my sister walked in on us during by the way) and let me drive without a license, and party. She was also the best hugger back then and for a long time after. It was like she created a monster, but after a while of me bugging her to end it with that asshole, she chose to end it with me and stay with him. That was another lesson I learned and had seen for years to come, WTF is with women and going with and staying with the biggest losers, abusers, and dick headed fuckers? I know about all that bad boy attraction bullshit but c'mon! That's ok...her friend Beth, who came to my class with her, heard about us breaking up and we fooled around in her kitchen a little, but me being Mr. Morals, didn't go further. I had, I guess a glow and behavior change because I was attracting everything after that "relationship", I started to have a few "Relations" with only those I really cared for too, that was very few and never used any female then for that, I repeat, back then, lol.

I was everybody's friend or at least friendly to everyone I came across from a simple "hey" to handshakes or high fives. I was the mayor on the island of misfits my younger brother would tell me. He and I guess all the others in school would not understand and made fun of the fact that I paid attention to what society called the ugly, nerdy, and just the perfect poster children for the title "misfit". One or two of my little friends were quite the shadows. I did not mind but if it interfered with my getting a girl, yeah, that's when I did. This entourage of misfits also did not help my situation with "John" and his buddies. I was targeted enough, and this just added fuel to the fire, but I just said fuck it, my problem and choice. The wall of us "Wangs' ' became stronger by number because of my being nice to them and kind of being their leader or idol. They did not have the same talents as my original first wave group, but still participated, so they were welcomed friends. Later, they became the best witnesses to what was to come. Some of the additions to my group were a few Vietnamese kids that I guess you could say were part of a program or exchange, but I met their adoptive families whenever they would invite me over. There were a few Hungs, a Hing, Tran, a Tun, etc. One of the funniest was Hing. This guy was an undercover badass! One day, that big black guy Rich I mentioned earlier, who liked to knee people, decided to verbally abuse and make fun of Hing in class. Hing warned him to knock it off, but Rich kept at him and started cat calling with waaa sounds and making fun of Hing's accent. I swear to all that is holy, that within 1 second, Hing smacked Rich 3 times with each hand and jumped-up kicking Rich back with both feet like a drop kick but without falling. Hing without one hint of losing breath, told Rich.."I fucking told you man, cut the shit!"..but funnier with broken accented English. I learned a lot of skills from these guys and realized what we call Martial Arts and must pay for and learn by going to a school, is what some cultures consider their street fighting and have been doing it since birth. One of the Hungs, studied Tae Kwon Do from a former master of mine, and was the mildest mannered quiet out of the bunch. He never liked when Hing would teach me the dirty words like most of us Americans learn first when learning a new language. I would joke and say out loud, something like No 'Du Ma' (No Fucking) ...in Vietnamese I learned from Hing, and Hung would look at me disappointed and say, this is bad...and I should not like this or think it's funny. I never wanted to offend him, and carried that for the rest of my life, making a better effort to learn more than just the funny or bad things to amuse others, but to understand all behind the cultures. "Everything is Kung Fu"

Senior Year!! Yey! Easy times, and great memory making. NOT!! For me anyway it was not a joyful experience because I cut and dicked around so much from Freshman through Junior year that I had to do a lot of work, attend, and make up assignments or extra ones given to pass. I found out the day I graduated, that I graduated, but I will get to that later, so let's go through the year and its events.

I still convinced the principal to let me run the intramural Self Defense Club with the same provisions. I also used the same "Advisor" Mr. C, who continued to add to the instruction. During the summer before I started senior year, some Chinese Kung Fu masters and apparently big movie stars in Hong Kong came to my county and were doing demos and lion/dragon dances type of parade there too. They wanted to open a Kung Fu school in my county. I was there like white on rice as one of their first students. There was an American assistant instructor with them, but I wanted to learn from the masters. I fell in love with that art so much, I went every night I could and mastered every form just to learn the next right away. After a while I asked one of my masters, who seemed to know more English, if he felt I was getting better? He looked me straight in the eye and said "You are good, but you are going to be very good one day" but he still did not let up on the hard work they put me through. I was now an official "Wang ". I had the Kung Fu pants, the earned Chinese symbol 3 button shirt and went to school that year with it on often like a cheese dick. It did give me more material to teach my fellow "Wangers". I still went to Kung Fu regularly and finally understood the balance and discipline of school, studies, work and working out, but not about being humble as far as my clothes advertising my martial arts. I understood that only after one guy, "Tito", who was a dickhead back then, but right by pointing that out. He later in life got into Federal Law Enforcement. I only know that because he was in my office later in life, but, like I said before, I will get to that. I started getting invited to a few House parties and met a girl "Sue" (for short) at one of them. She was Korean, and of course I heard the comments and questions about that from family members who questioned why I am so different in taste with everything. Different times than now, I still had growing pains from when my parents were my age, and Grandparents obviously influenced their way of thinking. Not racist, but typical sporadic comments, like, stereotyping. Sue joined me at the Kung Fu school too but did not take it as seriously as I did, and especially did not like that testing for the next ranks is charged a fee. She had a cool red Camaro and let me drive it often. I forgot why we ended it but I found out later she was with this volunteer firemen right after, maybe even during. We talked about marriage at one point but to tell you the truth, I think I liked the idea we were partners in Martial Arts, so I thought "why not be partners in life", and her being Asian was cool being a Kung Fu guy, a trophy wife, but also respecting the culture. Sick, but a true thought. She had issues about some Ex-boyfriend that she would make up being chased down from and had a very strict father who did not care what her interests were but told her that her place was to work the store he ran. For real, not stereotyping, but Typical and cliché. He told her she was a mistake, typical macho man "wants boy only" bullshit. Her brother pulled the same shit on her. That's enough of that. As I said earlier, everybody, no matter what culture, color or belief has beauty in them, and I saw it. I wish her well.

I was asked by the masters if I could be the "Bad Guy" in some instructional videos they were making that were sold in international magazines, one was a woman's Rape prevention and Self Defense video, and my co-star was a great martial artist who I would have done take after take with, if you know what I mean. When the videos were produced and sold, I had a set for myself and used them to advertise my instructors for a demo at the High School. I put a TV with a video cassette player in the Lobby for people to see what they can learn, and it helped my class develop too, but again, it also added more fuel to the fire for the (I assume) jealous asshole's behavior. Ok, enough of the introduction of a typical teenage life movie sob story, let's get into the shit sandwich that changed my ways.

I mentioned before that some dicks would come around and imitate us by striking poses and crying out with KIA! And other Kung Fu movie type noises, even right in the middle of my class space in front of me. This one I will call simply "Jay" was a slender but cut black kid who was talented at break dancing, and I would enjoy watching him doing his pop lock and moon walks and beat box stuff. Well, a few times he would be the one making fun of us, calling out and challenging but would be standing with that Hip Hop accepted buffalo stance and with one hand never leaving his balls. Seriously, it was like he could not let go, and when he did, the other hand would replace immediately. I had enough of the poses and interference and just redirected it toward him by grabbing my balls and the other hand repeating what he would say. "Yo Yo" and "what up?" and "Word" this and that. I guess I opened a whole bucket of shit because after school that day or after a few of those days, not sure of dates, he saw me after class and invited me to have a "talk". He put his arm around me and guided me down the hill path toward the Football/Baseball fields. I know what you are all thinking now, "Uh Oh! But no, I was so naive and still believed in the goodness of man that I went willingly. It was only when I noticed half the school following us that I got that feeling like in Jr. High when all the kids filled the walls to see a fight that I knew was coming. I was not" Hip" to understand what it meant when a guy asks "Wassup" with a finger in your face, so, like a wise ass I would answer "Not much how are you?" he would again ask louder "No Man, I said Wassup?" Then he went from open fingers in my face to an instant fist hitting my mouth. I smiled and tried to shake his hand to congratulate him on getting a shot in on me and that was enough. Nope, he continued to jab at me. I was such a cheese dick TV show. I took off my shirt, so did he, so being the topper I was, I then took off my sneakers like in class to teach the "evil doer" a lesson. Didn't happen. He jabbed me so fast and ducked all mine. He took my hardest spinning kick in his stomach and just smiled and brushed it off. I knew then, I sucked, and all the trophies and belts and competitions and such did not mean shit right then and there. I never knew what it felt like to get hit or to really fight without it being for near miss points. 'Jay" decided to crucify me by taking off his belt with the buckle spelling his name and put it across my back for all the sins I committed against him. I ran. I ran so fast that I could have beat any marathon runner or half back there was in the world. I went to the bathroom and looked in the mirror and I saw my face was so bad, I thought the mirror was loaned out from a funny house with how warped my face was. It looked worse than "Rocky" and was a mix of pepperoni pizza and roadkill. Can you fucking believe some female friend of "Jay's came in the bathroom while I was splashing my face to see just a little bit out of my eye and yelled at me about how upset "Jay" was and why did I push him to fight?? WTF?? I admitted that I made fun of him as much as he did me but really?? "Get the fuck outta here!" I said. Yeah, that's right, NY style, "outaa" I said. The head of the PT department, Mr. D, came in and saw me and asked what happened. It was after school, so no nurse was on duty. He sat me in his office and gave me an ice pack and called my parents. I thought I was dead meat when my father would find out I had a fight at school. I forget the ride home, if it was from my mother or someone else but man did my mother go off about it. She yelled at all the staff on the phone that there was left to yell at like Mr. D, not knowing that there was a fight and seeing half the school heading down to the field, like duh Mr. D… WTF? I don't remember talking to any principal staff that day if they were there. My mother obviously called my father because he was home a lot earlier than he usually is from his office. I did not get into it earlier and did not do much, but my late father was an FBI agent, and the best. I do not say that because of being his son, it is a fact. He did not deserve the way he died (Parkinson's disease), but like I said, RIP dad, I love you. Here is proof of how good he was at interviewing and interrogation but most of all, how great of a dad he was. My father always came home through the kitchen steps, like most of us, and had the same routine of going straight to his room, undoing his tie at a minimum then coming out in a white T-shirt and regular pants with belt and sitting at the dinner table head chair. I was in my room thinking of how embarrassed I was and the shame of showing my face to him caused by being tricked into going down to a field with that guy thinking it was really a "talk". Most of all, it was for losing the fight when I tried to defend myself. Sometimes after, I didn't think I really did try, because I did not want to break "The rules" so I half assed it to keep him off me and my strikes were always counter not attack mode, but I still failed and ran. I was thinking about the last time my dad was proud of me was maybe when I would win a ribbon for a race at the FBI sponsored picnics, he would take us too where his agent buddies, some like uncles to me were with their kids and I missed that kind of pride I would see rarely from him. Just then in the middle of my reflections, there was that call again of my name, but not in a yelling tone. I made the walk of shame to the dinner table and sat down without looking up for a while. My father asked me to look at him. I didn't want to, but you just do not disobey my dad. I saw the nod followed by a sigh from him. I could not tell right away if it was of disgust or of sympathy by just the expression on his face until he asked me what happened. I gave him the short BS version that this guy attacked me right away in front of the school, leaving out the whole trip down the hill and being tricked. He stood up, leaned against one of the walls with just his hand extended and looked up to the ceiling as if to absorb and think about what I just told him. My father simply put this to me next. "Terrence, sometimes people, when telling a story or their version of it, may leave out some or a lot of details that I would find out later are important, because they feel they would get in trouble, be embarrassed, or let me know that they did or said something that maybe led to or caused the incident. I am not saying you did but tell me again where and exactly step by step what happened."

I was blown away at how he knew something more and thought he would take it as a compliment when I said" that's exactly what's going on and I left out something." He was not amused at all or took my compliment well. He cannot stand lies no matter the reason or how little. I told him the truth and he then came to me, caressed my face and said he never meant that I should let anyone do that to me when he said do not fight in school. I could see the disappointment in his eyes when I told him that I did not want to or could not fight back effectively and that the kid was scratch free. All those years of holding back and just learning poses and forms and BS near miss point system fighting came to this moment of awakening, that I needed better and more. There was a line in the movie "The Last Dragon" where the little brother asked the main character 'Leroy' and my dad actually asked the same thing (in his own way.) "What good is all that Kung Fu jive, if you can't even use it?" the kid asked 'Leroy'.

The next day, my father brought me to the Police station after we went back to the school and approached the coaches and Principal about the fight. All the cops and chief knew who my family was and especially my father. I guess my father took away the belt buckle used on my face and body, from the school staff that found it in the field somewhere. He threw it down on the police officer's desk that was taking the report. Photos of my face and body were taken and the spelling of the kid's name was clearly visible on my back and side from the buckle. Nothing came of the report because it was written off as a mutual fight. There was nothing mutual about it. It was clear that it was time to do something myself to avoid this happening again to me or anyone. Back to old school superheroes. I almost gave up the Self Defense club, because it was a joke to most after I just showed that I failed to defend myself. "MR. C" the other instructor and advisor took me to the side and asked me "why didn't you take him out Tiger?" I never heard that term "Take him out" much before that, but it did ring in my ear from that point on. He told me and vowed it will not happen again if I give up the BS I was doing, and study under him. I did. This put such a surge of anger, and determination in me, I went back to the old school way of doing the minimum in academics, just enough to get by and focus on full time hand to hand no joke, throat chopping, combat and revenge. Batman, and Sir Galahad were back.

One day soon after my "Event", A friend got slammed down to the curb from a tall gork of a kid just for wearing a pink shirt. He had to be hospitalized and the teachers did nothing. Da da da Daaaaaaa!! Hero Terry to the rescue.! I found that kid and approached him about it and he told me to fuck off or I am next. I spun around him, jumped up and put that fucker in a sleeper hold that made him go out right away. Every class in the hallway filled with kids coming out to see the new me, the defender, the tough one, the superhero they should know and never doubt again. A teacher convinced me to let him go and wake him up. I asked him where the fuck was he and what did he do when this kid put my buddy in the hospital, NOTHING! Talk time is over! I got suspended for five days instead of 13 days, because I lied and said the kid attacked me first and I simply ducked and tried to hold him for a teacher. I told them what he did to Sebastian, everyone knew it and he must have thought I was going after him, so he attacked me first. Suspended? wooo! big deal but badass.

"A coward dies a thousand deaths; a hero dies but once."

(William Shakespeare-Act 1. Scene 2, line 32, Julius Caesar)

I will paraphrase parts from an article written by Jesse Enkamp. (KARATEbyJesse) by saying,

"Whatever path we choose, it will involve acknowledging and accepting that there will always be this gap, or battle, or Devil, or inner voice, or Resistance, or Ego, or whatever you want to call it, to haunt you. The question isn't "How do we stop this battle" anymore, the question is "How do we bridge the gap?" Because if we don't, we will keep dying over and over again."

"The Way" "Do" in Karate- "Tao" in Kung Fu is the path you choose to handle it. Some do it physically (Through movement). Some do it mentally (Through introspection) and some do it spiritually (Through beliefs)"

"The way doesn't matter, as long as you don't stray from it."

I strayed from "The Way" and did so over and over in my life, and some will say that is human nature, and one day I would find My Way.

Chapter Three

"THE REAL KARATE KID STORY"

I mentioned earlier that I was invited to house parties. I lost my train of thought with that and talked about a girl; don't you hate when that happens? I was asked to watch the door at one as sort of a bouncer. I had the reputation of fighting back and not taking shit. One buddy of mine "Tom" was also friends with the dark side if you will, like "John" and them, but was cool with me and knew my brothers and their rep. sure enough, eventually 'John' came to the door with the usual one liner bully crap and with the usual ass crowd that shadowed him. He brushed by me and got himself a beer and yelled out, "what the fuck are you doing here Devine" you fuckin pussy, like you can bounce?", I looked up and said for the first time in my life to him "Fuck you John" with finger No more than a second later he and his buddies swarmed on me in a huddle not knowing I ducked down to the floor and crawled out. It was a move straight out of a movie or cartoon cloud watching them rumble in a rugby match amongst themselves with kicks too, but I was not there or hurt. My buddy "Tom" , a huge kid, also not knowing I was fine, came yelling my name and to the rescue, throwing every one of those guys in the air to get to me, but I was behind him and fine. That is no shit and funny, I don't care who you are. You know, I said this all my life and I still do to this day, that "That some guys you look at, and automatically you can tell that they are a dick. 'John' was one of them. The waiting was over, the bully finally showed he was willing to go that extra step and touch me. He will soon find out that was a big mistake. There was never going to be another beating on me from anyone ever again. Mr. nice guy was gone and dead and a fucking Ninja developed in me. Holy shit! That just fucking reminded me of some other asshole. How can I fucking forget? ok, this is no shit either so get ready for this crap. Rewind a little!

Around sophomore year, this Russian kid "Alex" came to our school. I didn't recognize him at all so I knew he had to be the new kid. I saw him in the study hall reading a book on Ninjutsu. Yeah, exactly what I thought, WTF? I just looked at him to the point that he finally looked up at me and kind of confusingly said what's up? I introduced myself and told him my name. He said he knew who I was. I invited him to join our club since he obviously was into Martial Arts or at least interested in reading about it. He declined but we became sort of associated friends. A while went by that year, and I noticed a change in behavior in one of my friends toward me. His name is Ralph. Great student and practitioner back then. He sort of had this questioning wise-ass type of cockiness suddenly during Defense class after school like my stuff was bullshit. I finally had enough and asked him if I did anything wrong like a bitch. He said that this Russian kid 'Alex' could probably take me and that I was full of shit, and so were my styles according to his opinion. Now, I do not normally care what people think, but this behavior spread to even a female or two that were like shadows of mine as I described earlier, and they went to the "dark side" too. I was not having it, so I approached 'Alex' , and told him to stop talking shit, brainwashing my friends, and any time he felt "froggy," Jump!. He challenged me to a (straight out of a movie) "Ninja death match." WTF is wrong with this mother fucker? That was funny and stupid enough to even hear never mind the fact he had a second man to take his place if he could not continue, it would be my friend Ralph. I agreed just to humor his ass, and picked a second as a joke, my other buddy Chris to be my second and I named my old elementary school as the meeting place so I could go home to dinner quickly when we were done. We both agreed no weapons allowed. This asshole showed up in full Ninja battle rattle, mask and all and knelt and did the whole ritual. "Rin," all the way through "Zen" ("The Ninjitsu levels of power" symbolized by hand and finger positions) what a fucking cheese dick. I did see at the end he spread his arms apart with the fingers positioned in an added level that meant, "To the death". That is when I knew he was fucking serious. It was America Vs. Russia, White Ninja magic against the Black dark magic. 'Alex" came at me from across the field full sprint and jumped in the air with an obvious flying kick that I had maybe two days to block or get out of the way from, so I did. I threw one punch. Followed by a roundhouse kick to his head and he was down. He knelt there in his original prefight power pose "Rin" finger position, and was breathing in hard like he was recharging, but I knew it was pure pain and embarrassment. He stood up and threw a fast reverse punch (cross) to my chest. The one and only strike I let him get. I had enough of this shit, I grabbed him, took his mask off, and choked the shit out of him until he tapped and bowed down to submit. Nope, not the end yet sports fans. This fuck face suddenly pulled a fucking chain out of his pants, that I guess was taped to his leg and started doing the whole swinging BS like he was leading a horse. I do not get scared, I get pissed at liars and cheaters, so I ran right into that shit, it wrapped around my wrist, and I took that shit away so fast I think I hurt his hand that he held it in. He submitted again before I could whip him. I told him and especially Ralph, that if they ever want to test me again, they can learn more for 20 years, come back, and I will still kick their asses even if I sat on mine for all that time. I will talk about one other incident about Alex later in life. Back to school now. Ralph and I made contact a few times, and we are fine with each other. We were kids after all.

I said earlier that I started to cut school again a little, still did my work, but was not focused as much as I should be, especially when it came to girls. What a fucking distraction. I never had a dry spell after "Di or Sue. I had a few "sessions" with a couple of different one's but met this one chick "Camille" that had a body of a stripper and the loudest, horniest sexually aggressive I had back then. My high school was considered "South" while hers was "North" and was quite a trip by car, bike, minibus, however I could, never mind by foot, but man, it was worth it. I told you before this is not going to be a teenage movie, but I will put it this way, I never had to do any work and Camille would smack my hands away if I tried to even assist in the rhythm. She oiled her body to make those tight pants slip on where you could 'read lips" if you get my meaning. It is obvious that she really could not get enough, unfortunately, not from me only, anyway. With that, the next thing I will discuss is what I talked about earlier about trusting women and their stories. Mind fuckers.

Ok so here it is, the start of the bullshit that women do. I "went out" with Camille for a little while longer during the year. I even took some modern jazz shit at a hall just to be with her, but I was good at that and most dancing because of my brothers letting me club with them. I got a phone call from her one night that happened to be the same night I had turned her down from meeting at a club we teens went to regularly. She sounded like she was crying after being silent for a while, like she was testing if I had known anything, or something was wrong. When I asked for the thousandth time what is going on, she said 'some guys" tool her around to the back of the club and raped her. She knew some of the names because they hit on her in the club originally and big shock, there was the name of Coyle, the last name of the prick that went after my brother to get to me I mentioned earlier. I knew the other names but did not have problems with them...yet! I threw the phone down and screamed my ass off and got my father's attention quick and demanded that he call someone, and that "My girlfriend was raped". My father looked at me and did not even get out of his chair. He told me to sit down and listen. He asked me "where was she? When did I see her last? How does she know these guys? Etc. For the first time, I yelled at my father and told him to stop questioning her and do something. He went to the kitchen and picked up the phone and asked me all those questions he asked me. She just asked to talk to me, so I did and assured her I would do something if the police did not. This is the part that I should have realized that something stank, like BULLSHIT up my nose. She told me not to call the police, that she did not want to do anything about it because she was afraid and asked me if I believe her and if I love her, I will not question her decision. Well, the Ninja man superhero was in full effect. I called my friend Chris to pick me up and take me to where I knew one of the asshole's living areas, a few minutes away. I knew this one had a brand-new car he loved and always took care of, like I said, took care of, whoops! Something happened that night, like a Big orange cloud in the sky lighting up the dark ninja night or should I say "Knight". This is what I "Heard About" anyway..lol. The next day at school, I saw Coyle between periods, and I saw he was turning sick from fear. He asked if he could talk to me. I looked at him like he was crazy, and I think I asked that at the same time out loud. He said that he did not know what I was told but that Camille invited them all to the back of the club and gave them all blowjobs as well as having 'DP" ("Double penetration" for you virgins), at the same time. I was more upset at believing this than I was about him telling me. He was begging with respect like a servant on a Kung Fu flick asking for mercy from the master. I did believe it and believed his sincerity and told him "Ok" thanks.

I called her right away to tell her off, no answer. I cut school early to go to the North and found her in the parking lot with arms around this big fuck face I knew from football as a kid Brian. This was a gross mutant looking mother fucker who hung around other losers known to use and abuse women and just drink and smoke weed as well as other drugs. I ran so fast toward her the wind made me tear, which I was anyway from the sight of this bitch with him a day after claiming rape and questioning my love? Hell fucking no! I yelled her name, and she must of shit her pants because she let him go and put her hands quickly into her back pockets like she was holding it in. Brian stepped in front of her and said "WTF you doin here Devine? yeah he said doin? I did not misspell shit so don't correct me. I asked him "How does my dick taste in your mouth there buddy, or better yet, I said while looking at her with disgust, "How does four guys dick taste in your mouth?" he tried to get tough but was more confused than anything. I let him in on the whole thing, but he denied it all and said bullshit and told me to get outa here! Shut up, he said "outa here" for real. I called her about everything in the book and asked her what about Brian? Like…are you going to really BS him and stay with him after you clearly don't know how to have a relationship with one? She had the balls to use the word 'love' and told me "But I love him Terry " and it's over between us. Duh?? Right there Brian should have at least picked up on the fact she just admitted being with me, never mind 4 others, but he was too fucking stupid or hard up to realize or care she is a fucking slut bag scum waffle. The day was still young, and I went back to mine to finish the day and teach after school.

I guess I should have stayed out of school because sure fucking enough, after class, when I left the lobby doors that lead outside the front of the school, more trouble came my way. It went like this. I spotted a friend of mine waiting for her sister while parked at the curb playing with her dog. I squatted to pet the dog and was chatting with her when suddenly, a loud screech of car brakes right behind me startled me and my friend. It was the chicken fucker who "Had issues with his other car" the night I got the call from the "victim of his rape". My friend picked up her dog and got into her car and sped off when she saw him running at me yelling my name along with some cursing and saying that I am dead! He tried to tackle me but since I was already squatting and it was too late to stand by the time he got to me, I rolled back and put my feet in his chest, sending him over me in a tumble. He yelled that I "blew up his car." I denied it and I still will, so nice try audience, lol. I warned him to back off and that I did not know what he was talking about. Apparently, Coyle, the one that told me the truth, must have told him that this bitch was my girlfriend and that I looked like I was upset and did not believe him, so I guess he put two and two together and it was me as the answer. He came at me again with some jabbing, so I spit in his face and jabbed him right back. A nerdy, ``Wimpy from

Popeye" looking teacher that I knew only from association came out and that's where the beautiful acting and set up came from 'Ghost Rider,' (Fire joke). He yelled for me to get the fuck off him and told the teacher I am crazy and coming after him and such. The teacher said he saw me jabbing, and that he is a witness. I couldn't believe my ears. I went off and told the prick that I will kill him if he ever tries hurting me again or any of my friends or family. The teacher again tried warning me to stop the threats. I walked off and knew this was not the end.

My father was a hardworking, God fearing great Irish catholic man, who I understand was raised hard and cold. That aspect, I will not dwell on. I say this now because this will be the ultimate test of his patience with me and how to handle certain behavior I showed; most of the behavior was unintentionally displayed and found out by him. He already proved to be one that understood behavior, thoughts, and can sniff the truth or a lie whether you were in front of him or not. That made him great at his job and as a father. He was right about my fight scenario (version 1) I talked about earlier and showed patience to listen again. He was right about the "Rape" intuition he had about it being false claim and now he will once again ask me for the truth about this kid and the car.

It was the same night that this prick attacked me that he called my house and asked to speak to my father. Thank God I answered and denied him the request and warned him not to call again. He did, more than 5 times in a row. My father asked me what the hell is going on and why am I telling someone not to call again. At first, he thought it was a girl I was fighting with but then he picked up when I could not get to the phone on time. He listened and just looked at me with the typical I am going to kill you expression. My father just told this asswipe to call back in a minute after he "Has to get me "excuse to get a recorder he used for taping calls at work I guess, the suction cup on receiver type and it plugged into the recorder. He called back and we had him on loudspeaker, and he told my father I blew up his car and he wants payback for it financially. My father asked him of course for proof and how do you know and the usual. He stated, "It was about a girl that I think your son was dating and he set my car on fire." My dad looked at me like he knew exactly what this was and just listened and told him to go ahead and call the police if he wants but he has no proof and not to call back unless it is with his parents. Fuckface called back anyway knowing I may answer. I left the recorder and device on the phone and taped the conversation. My father told me it is legal if one party involved directly with the situation (case) has knowledge that recording is going on. These were many lessons my father taught me when I showed interest. I will get to that later. I was directly involved. This clueless fucktard kept saying that 'I will handle you" and again "You will get yours" and that I will be "taken care of" I finally asked him how he plans on doing that and he simply said that "he will do it himself as simple as that" Not exactly the best thorough threat I ever received but I felt it was enough. My father called the local Police in response to this, and a female cop showed up. I recognized her from being around the county. Yes readers, she was hot and during the conversation I realized I knew her from a club me and my brothers went to that got me in. She questioned the legality of the taping, and I of course opened my big legal jive my dad taught me and said it was directly involving me and the guy so fuck him and what is she going to do. My father shut me up quickly. She asked me if I did have anything to do with the car being on fire. My father told her, and I jumped on the same fact that this is not what we called her for, we wanted to report the threat and that's it. So, take notes trick and get the fuck out and question the prick. She took my statement and went to his house and took his. A while later, she then came back stating the same shit and asked me again why he thinks strongly that I did this. I had nothing to say so unless I am formally charged, fuck off and see you at the bar ho.

This is all I needed. All by senior year, I got a Ninja after me and brainwashing friends, a home boy's name on my body from a belt buckle, I got the swarm of John and his bully buddies always fucking with me and actually willing to finally get physical, assholes after my brother to get to me, a lying sack of shit slut bullshitting me to the point I "Could have went" Ninja, that was the second time I got my heart crushed BTW and now in addition to the scum waffle family, this douche and a cop thinking I did it, as well as my dad now, What is next. I will tell you.

Some time went by, and I lived day by day staying clear of the scum squad. One night when I thought things blew over, my dad called me into his room after dinner. I knew I saw a look or two from him during dinner but thought maybe he was waiting for me to say something wise when he was picking on my younger brother about some nonsense. I did get kind of brave in those days and mouthed off to him to back him off. Getting back to being summoned to his room, I went very slowly with a thousand thoughts in my head of what it could be about. He did that thing again where he looks up in thought while he leans against a wall with his arms folded looking like he is having a serious headache. I asked what's up? My own father asked me if I wanted to go to jail? and he was the one to lock me up? WTF dad? I thought to myself. I acted confused until he whipped out a certain list I put together and had hidden in my room behind my wall unit. Here we go, Mr. FBI strikes again knowing me too well or at least wanting to. This list was what I called and titled like an idiot "My Death List". I named every motherfucker who ever messed with me and rated their safety from me or order of what they would get in return by putting stars next to their names (1 to 5 stars) of course the more stars, the bigger the asshole you are and the more punishment you will get from me if not dead. My dad decided to give me a quick lesson in psychological forensic behavior study. He pointed out that if I was brought in, some quack would point out the stars, the pressure I made writing, the colors I chose and the order of the whole list and I would end up in a straight jacket or in jail. I could not deny shit about making the list and just when I was about to Bullshit about it being old, he said "don't even think about telling me you forgot this existed because sure fucking enough, there was the (new asshole's name) added. I told my father that yeah, I was angry and was planning on just beating them up that using the name "Death List" was just an expression. I thought I was clear and out of it, but then guess fucking what? NOT!

Good old dad saved all kinds of shit, from coins to sports cards and even newspapers from great events like the first shuttle and man on the moon kind of shit. Just my luck, dad decided to keep some more newspaper articles about certain guys found hanging by their underwear on telephone poles. This apparently happened to a few of them and always made the paper in a blog the Police put out publicly. My dad asked me while grinning with clenched teeth and a pointing finger "Is this you?" Did you do this? I looked at the blog, read it all and caught myself smiling until my dad woke me from my satisfaction and stoked look. When I looked at him, there was no need to answer, he made up his mind and I could see that when his mouth dropped, and eyes widened. He then just asked the last question that was too early at that point in my life to answer. I will say it again, only at that point in my life. He asked, "Would you really kill someone?" I looked down in thought like I needed a minute and looked right at him and just shrugged and replied honestly with no expression that "You just never know". "Looks like something out of a Bruce Lee movie to me dad. huh?"

I was put on a tight leash after all that. Real shock huh? I was also suddenly required to get all assignments and homework received in class and signed on all ends, parents and teacher. One teacher, my English class one had regular communication with my mother. I think she must have been my sibling's teacher because she had the most patience with me. There was one time she was discussing how we should get in the habit of reading novels. At least one a week outside the curriculum to open our minds and imaginations up. My father also harped on reading a newspaper every day to stay up on current events and have something to discuss with someone in common whether it be sports, politics or anything I would be able to mutually participate in besides Martial Arts. My mother said I was a horse with blinders on and never saw outside my own world. The English teacher asked me once, "What was the longest story or novel I read," I could tell by her expression and smirk, that she expected an answer like, a comic book or a "Bruce Tegner" book on Karate. I told her I read "SHOGUN" which is one of the thickest books right up there with "The Art of War". She looked at me with glasses tilted down on the bridge of her nose with the biggest expression of disbelief and c'mon written all over her face until she asked, no told me, "There is no way you read the whole book of SHOGUN at your age and level now." I told her that she is fully aware of my interests in Martial Arts and all that go with it as well as its cultures and language. I asked her in Japanese if she understood. "(Wakarimasu ka?)" She opened her eyes wide in amazement, smiled in amusement eyebrows raised and hand on hip, and spoke Japanese back answering that yes, she understood and thank you for sharing." (Hai, rikai shite kyoyu shite itadaki arigatogozaimasu)" Then nodded with eyes closed and a satisfaction impressed smile. Yeah, have that cup of Shut the Fuck Up teach!..lol. Getting back to the arrangement, this made it so I could not cut, claim no homework and study so no more extra shit after I taught Self Defense, without permission. They wanted to take that away too, but this was my baby, and no one was going to run my class and disappoint others. I was in a real rut. I ran away for about 2 days, stayed with whoever was willing to help, even in their basement. Two people who really befriended me during the year were Trevor and his girlfriend, who he always claimed he would marry. No, I never saw it happening either. She played mind and heart games on him and as soon as I would look her in the eye, I knew she still had some wildness in her and could never bullshit me. On the side of that BS, they were great friends and were there when I had issues at home to listen and even let me stay over when I pulled that teenage runaway bullshit on my family. I decided to ask permission to have a demonstration of my club in the auditorium when the whole school could be there. I was granted permission to do the demonstration. I was great at breaking shit, and forms and fighting finally. I was going to break a brick like I have done at home many times. The students did their Karate and Kung Fu forms I taught them, they did some one step sparring, and did some weapons I showed them the basics on. All was great until I was due for the grand finale. It was my turn to break this brick with the other two bricks holding it. It fucking toppled over and broke right before the curtain opened. Holy shit! I looked to the side backstage freaking out knowing that in a minute, the whole school would be watching me, including the bullies, the pricks, the assholes old and new and would finally see what I could do and what their face could end up as, but I was fucked. I was in such a rush I just put the fucking thing back together evenly along its crack to mold it like it never broke and carefully placed it on the holding two bricks. I looked at Trevor and his girl again and could only shrug and laugh. They looked so heartbroken and disappointed but oh well, it was show time and I would deal with them later. The curtain opened, I had my eyes closed like I was meditating but I was really praying it would not fall and break again. The bell rang and the students started moving and yelled, "Break that shit already!" I opened my eyes wide and smashed that shit so hard, another piece of it broke off like it wasn't broken at all, but the loose pebbles went in my hand and the students thought the yell was my KIA!. Haaaaaaa. It was me seeing the blood and feeling the pain of that shit in my hand. I bowed and they went nuts and cheered with a loud YEAH!!! Clapping and all, ..Suckers. I made up for it later though because there is always that one asshole and hater that wants to see it for real up close and dare me and just make sure it was not an act. The same motherfucker that tripped on the frozen mud at my house when we were kids looking at the burglar in the window, yeah that pussy. He had someone hold the leftover brick I left on stage for cleanup. I told him it takes just as much talent for the holder as well as the breaker to assure success in the breaking part of Martial Arts.

Though that worked, nope, still dared me and assured he would hold it solid. He leaned into it holding that brick underhand at the right angle and WHAM! I hammer fisted that fucker so hard with fear of failure, embarrassment, and adrenaline that I cracked it where you could just pull it apart. I was so cocky I told him that if it was a solid hold, it would have gone all the way through like on stage. lol. I was such a dick. The whole philosophy of this demonstration working in my favor against the bullies did not go according to plan. In fact, it brought them on strong with more challenges verbally, more waaaaa!! Sounds during my class and typical fuck face behavior on their part. Ok, readers, we finally made it, the end of the High school drama, but wait, there is more. John and maybe only two of his buddies walked by me near the principal's office that was connected to the lobby. John purposely did the old shoulder brush against me. That was it. I had enough of this piece of shit. I turned around, saw him laughing and looking back at me. I took my hand and wiped my shoulder and smiled at him like I was wiping shit off me. I turned back to walk down the hall and sure fucking enough, here is Captain Shitface, flying and jumping behind me to ask, "What was that Devine?" want to get your ass kicked and all the usual boring threats, I was so used to hearing after all these years I finally said "Sure" "give it a try and see what happens". I could see the shock in his face when I talked back like he just got slapped. He was not used to me being tough with him. He took me by the throat and smashed me against the wall. I smiled and said, "Thank you". He was even more surprised now. "What the fuck you mean thank you? You are a fucking idiot". I then simply told him "Thank you for finally touching me and giving me a reason to take you out." I could tell he was really registering what was going on and what I said, just by his expression and mine being so calm and smiling during it all. The principal came out and asked, "what is going on and where do we belong?" I told him" Nothing I cannot handle and will". I was in such a rage when John walked away scratch free from me, my hand started shaking and I had to control it by making a fist and holding it down. The students witnessing it all did the usual "ooooooohhh" that they always do when they see a fight, hear tough talk arguments or even public kissing. lol. Ok this was it, as promised. John found me later that same day at my locker and knocked down my books like a typical wimp Vs. bully after school special on TV. I looked around and then smiled at him. He said, "What the fuck do you keep smiling for?" I said, "because this is the first time you had the balls to come to me alone". I walked towards him and said, "let's go". "C'mon asshole! Let's go" I said again. He had his eyebrows up in confusion, his speech was choked up, cracked in voice and so faint in disbelief. He was moving backward and losing his footing and would just kind of say "C'mon?" back with more of a question than a statement. I was now the aggressor, and he could not even throw a good punch. After all these years, he just could swing for the fences with a punch that once again, I had two days to block. I tripped him with one sweep while grabbing his shirt. I put him down on the floor of the hallway and just punched him once to submit him and get his attention and realize that I was able to kill him at any point. I didn't. I could not believe that this was it, the time I thought about for years that I would rehearse all mighty "what if?" That was finally here in front of me, and this is all it took? A sweep and a punch and done? Hell fucking no, I had to get those rehearsed lines off my chest. I told him that "I spared his life many times." "I never hated someone so much in my life to the point I could taste it" "The last thing you will see is my smiling face as you fade off" and all sorts of borrowed lines like that. I was not satisfied but fuckit, I thought it was over finally, so I let him go and all I heard was a lot of "Holy Shit" chants like I was at a Pro wrestling match. Late lunch period came, and I sat in the lobby with the "Wangs". I was sitting there waiting to hear from my friends about what they might have heard from the usual fast rumor control around the school of me beating up my lifelong bully. I had nothing to say and just knew something was not right or satisfying. I was waiting for the principal to have the loudspeaker trick call my name to the office with the "You are in trouble" introduction. It goes like this. "Mr. Terrence Devine, it is in your best interest to report to the principal's office immediately". Not like I have ever heard that before, wink. I felt all the eyes and whispers around me, on top, sides, everywhere knowing that I was the talk of the school, but I also felt a dark cloud. I heard my friends asking each other the same shit they heard, and I even glimpsed and saw them imitating my moves used to defeat the evil doer. I told them to stop because everyone including and especially on top of us, yeah, that click, was watching to see if I was bragging or cocky about it. I did not feel that way at all and was really upset not knowing what would come of it. Well, the devil must have heard my thoughts because here comes the footsteps of more evil doers. The gang of defending dickheads, the barrel of bullies ready to confront me with their ringleader of the circumcised circus of suckers, John himself. The scenario played in my head of how it was going to go down. A couple of my friends jumped up like straight out of a Chinese movie with poses like they were ready to yell "Right!!" and fly kick in the air to defend me. I told them to sit down. I looked at all these motherfuckers and asked them one thing "Are you really going to risk your lives for this piece of shit when you know he is wrong and our history" No response, just some "cccccc yeah rights" and challenge words of "common!" Yeah, I spelled that one right because he said it right for once. I warned them I was "not going to have any mercy and that it will just be me and leave my friends alone, they have nothing to do with it. " Right out of a comic book I swear. One of my "Wangers", I forget who said would say to me "Terry, there are like 7 of them," like I didn't fucking know. I told them to sit down again. John must've thought I was going to get up right there and then because he pressed his legs and weight forward leaning against my legs blocking me from standing up. His groin was right in my face so guess what? Nuff said! Whack! and grab and pull down he goes. Next! Oh, look, that guy is not protecting his clavicle. Smash! Down he goes. It continued with each one of them. I never said I would not get hit or thrown and pushed and pulled back and forth. I was hit and tackled and kicked but I will tell you this, I was fucking "Miyagi" at the end standing over their broken asses, ribs, arm or two, and nose when it was all over. I was back to that crying voice I had when I hit that nun back in fourth grade, and said, "Don't ever let me have to do that again". I looked up while walking away and noticed what appeared to be the whole school looking at me with the assistant principal and staff holding everybody back. The assistant principal put his arm around me and said, "Let's go Terry" "I knew it had to come to this, we tried everything else, detention, parent talks, suspension so we will work this out". Ten day suspension was how they worked it out and told my parents. My folks were fuming at first about what happened, and it was allowed until the principal told them "We tried everything else, it happened fast and with too many to break up and Terry still used more restraint than we would have given the history between him and those kids." He put that in writing later in life. I know this because when I went for one of my first Law Enforcement jobs, I had to explain the suspensions for fighting, so there it was in my file. Wooo!! Chalk one up for Principalnator!. Now those fuckers and everyone to follow knew what I could do, finally. I waited like the fucking Taliban.

I had enough, no more Mr. Nice guy as the saying goes. No more goody good, no more do not hit first rule BS, or talk. It was now going to be the dark side. For about a week or two, I broke about ten Glass windows that were in the middle of the heavy doors you go through at some stairwells and ones that lead outside. I was obviously dimed out because just as I was going for another, I caught one of the maintenance guys quickly press back to hide on the other side and nod to his coworker like a warning I was coming. I pushed the bar down to open the door slowly and told them to have a nice day...suckers. My venting was over.

During any breaktime, especially summer, I would go with my family trips that my late uncle Kevin, a priest but retired Colonel from the US Army would invite us on. Many different places domestically but also overseas. Anywhere From Italy to Medjugorje (Former Yugoslavia) for religious pilgrimages to just plain old travel vacation fun. That was a very few times but great experiences. I mostly took advantage of break time to go hang with friends, work out at multiple Martial Art studios my buddies were part of and meet more local instructors and friends of theirs. I met two twins Karl and Pierre, and a guy named Tom. Never asked his last name but that would come into play soon, and funny. There was a local Instructor, Rubin who was teaching some Chi Sao (Sticky Hands) and knife dagger stuff too. I couldn't tell if some of the stuff I had seen Tom or Karl do was Wu Shu learned from Rubin's studio or they did it somewhere else. They were fantastic. We would sometimes go to the local teen type night clubs and enjoy the music and dancing and talk shop about our dreams or plans with our Martial Arts. Pierre, Karl's twin, who I never saw practice with and unaware if he did, told me that he knew how to run a business and they would open a school. That dream was fulfilled because later in life, I saw his school location, as well as Tom's opened my County, I grew up in.

I was quite the 'mall rat' and loved hanging at the arcade, hanging with some rough playing but nice enough fellow mall rats. I picked up a few fashion changes because of whatever was popular at the time to fit in. Parachute pants, fingerless suede or leather gloves, studded or not. One only if you were into Michael Jackson..lol.. I personally had an admiration and obsession with 'Prince' to the point I did lip sync contests or performances, including in school for a talent show instead of Martial Arts one time. I sang 'Beautiful Ones' that asks in its theme, of who the girl he is with wants. Is it going to be him? Or the other guy?It was something I was going through with my childhood friend turned girlfriend for a while, Molly, when either I found out or saw she was with someone else . Of course, that too was met with grief from the bullies who one named Anthony pulled the speaker plug out causing the music to stop but my microphone was still on. Everybody heard me ask if "This is some kind of

Fuckin Joke?". I finished with my own voice just fine and went to the bathroom in the lobby. Sure enough, in walks a laughing little buck tooth piece of crap Anthony, asking "What's the matter Devine, you, ok? ` ` and then came toward me. Well, let's put it this way, Prince wore heeled boots, and Anthony got to know the hard way, that I am thorough with my costumes." Boot to the head!" nuff said. That talent of costume attention to detail would come into play later with my undercover work.

Anyway, back to breaktimes. Although I had no school of my own to teach besides the program I ran in High school, I would put fliers out offering to teach privately. I stole so much verbiage from other schools to describe and make my style attractive. Didn't know what to call my style back then, with the mixture of Kuen Pai, Tae Kwon Do, Goju, etc..I simply called it 'The Devine Way of Self Defense' and had a Dove in the middle of a Yin Yang symbol as my logo to show a sort of fight for peace theme. It looked like a yellow duck, instead of a gold dove..lol. I had made t-shirts with the logo and title in the back that you would get ironed on at any novelty shop. Didn't have a cell phone back then of course so it was my home number which did not go over well with my parents having strangers' calls. One time, while either hanging at the mall or at the teen club, I met this one girl whose mom ran a print shop. She offered to make business cards with my name, logo and number to start. I appreciated the efforts and kindness she showed but eventually she became clingy and kind of obsessed psycho like. She confided one day to me that she was a "Good Witch". I of course just nodded and went along to humor her. I am reluctant to write this because to this day, after some shit she pulled and demonstrated, with witnesses I trust, I wouldn't be surprised if she came to my door as I speak asking WTF am I doing, although I have not seen her in over 35 years. Get this, ...one day after a tournament or demonstration of some sort we went to or held, a group of us like Myself, Chris from school, his girlfriend. And some others went to a Chinese Restaurant to celebrate. My buddy Chris liked to practice his Chinese he learned (I guess from his Chinese girlfriend) while ordering the food and chopsticks. Well, no shit...little miss 'Good Witch' gets up to go to the bathroom and tells me not to go anywhere because "You know I can find you" she said.

I said as I moved out of the booth to let her out "whatever", and to "stop with the BS 'I am a Witch shit." No more than a second after I sat down and nodded, rolling my eyes to my friends about her, the fucking saltshaker moves and tilts over falling in front of my eyes. I looked at everyone in shock and questioning expressions followed. I looked around to see if I pulled the tablecloth. Nothing! I looked around more and then straight to the bathroom hallway to catch a wink coming from my little psycho witch. She proudly nodded in satisfaction and then entered the bathroom. No Shit!

I also liked to hang out with friends on the other side of town closer to my home in front of the pizzeria or the movie theater. Back then it was a Grand Union or A&P that took up most of the lot. This is where some of my friends that did not go to my school hung out. Ones I knew through others or the mall or teen clubs. I was still a little egotistical asshole sometimes who would show off moves publicly with them, with play fighting etc. Without even thinking of repercussions, I would also throw little cheap or self-made metal 'Chinese or Ninja Stars' at vehicles that sped by, pissed me off, or just for the thrill of trying to pop their tires. I was just reminded recently about that from a childhood friend, David, that I caught up with on social media and now call regularly. He hung out with me at the mall, teen clubs, and definitely witnessed a lot of things I should be in jail for or see a priest about..lol. One day while hanging at the pizza place, Rocco's, a school friend invited me to go to his house since his parents were gone and hang out until more came to have a mini house party. These were not mall rat type friends and not part of my Wang Crew. These were the yuppy well to do but cool kids that were talented at different stuff. This buddy who was having me over, Phil, did not know my other friends or hang out with them. This was a last-minute decision to go with him too. I say this as a warmup for another No Shit moment. No more than an hour into this party, Phil comes to me and says my friend Chris, his girlfriend, and someone else hanging back in a car were asking for me at the door. I went outside and with an obvious confused look and voice I asked how the fuck did they know where I was and how to find me? Chris pointed to his car and there was Psycho Witch Bitch! Chris's girlfriend then yelled at me and asked me "Where is your sense of responsibility?'. I again asked What the fuck is going on. Chris said that the Good Witch gave verbal directions of where to find me, while he drove. This cuntolla sandwich told my friends that all withing just a few weeks, I had sex with her, she got pregnant and lost or aborted the baby and that I am ignoring her. I laughed my ass off, not amusing his girlfriend at all and told Chris to think about timeframes of what they are saying. First, no sex happened, I stopped seeing her after the restaurant ordeal. Second, how can someone be found pregnant, and abort 2 weeks later after hanging for the first time no longer than a meeting? They thought about it, and I could see they finally realized what I was telling them. But..this girl definitely had some kind of psychic power. I always preached that there is no other power but God, but this proved me wrong, again. I will not discuss her again except this one more example of proof. Over a decade later in the late 90s, my second wife went to a meeting of some kind of mothers or wives' group for something. She came home with an expression on her face of 'What the Fuck?' and asked me who this Witch was?" My heart dropped into my stomach, and I said, "No fucking way!" She told me when she took out a picture of me in my Dress Blues from my first term in the Army to show a girl next to her, whose man was also deployed, some girl from across the room stopped talking and stared straight at her and said, "That's Terrence Devine". No Shit!..it was her..the "Good Witch" once again years later still fucking around. Never again since, but I tell you what...nothing will surprise me if she knows I am writing as I speak.

One time at the mall, I was in front of the arcade we all hung out at, and one kid that I can't remember a name to, never mind a face asked me if I knew some guy named Clifford? I said no, why? Then he asked me if I really was good at my "Karate Shit" and that he needed help, that this guy Clifford was after him and left some friends of his laying on a lawn when he fought. I said I could ask around, and he could count on me to defend him if need be. I spotted my buddy Tom who knew Karl and Pierre. He was hanging around the railing overseeing most of the middle of the mall and figured he may know something. I told him the situation, and he smiled at me and said Clifford was his last name, just like Rich did in school that time when I heard about him but didn't know I was talking to the actual person. He looked at me with the same curious facial expression. He then said yeah, he was after the kid. He also asked me what my last name was. I told him, and he said he was asked to go after me too for some douche bag I fought. We were both told and sent after another without knowing our full names. We agreed it was BS and were cool with each other. Later in life, I even trusted my second oldest son Brandon under the teachings of Tom Clifford schools since I had missions away often or just not around to teach.

The rest of my free time was at the local public pool, near our High school (Germonds Pool) or some called it "Traphagen". I had a few scraps there. One was an asshole who laughed when my brother landed on his back after a dive causing pain, so I challenged him. First time I was ever hit hard in the nose enough to bleed all over, but I took it and spat on him and eventually it was broken up. Another was a little shit that got physical and abusive with Molly, my childhood friend I had relations with on and off. I spotted him and lectured him about using women and touching them against their will. He smiled and said "That's the American Way"

So, I showed him the "Devine Way" and throat punched that

fucker

Getting back to school: I had buckled down and returned to school with a vengeance to graduate and make up all the work and clean up the mess I made academically by doing whatever extra shit they had for me, staying after school, if need be, to help with projects, volunteer for any bitch boy errands, whatever. That reminds me. Have you ever noticed that those "Yuppy" stuck up "JAP" click types that work for the school yearbook or video always put their friends in 90 % of it all? All the "Biffs, Tads and Muffys' they could find, as comedian Robin Williams used to joke about. Ok, I aged myself there. Anyway, I had some great footage of my self Defense club and some poses with them, demo footage and all sorts of things I know they took and said they would use. They not only left out all that, and only put one picture of us that was in the beginning of the year with a lot of students missing, but they threw out all the unused footage and pictures I wanted to keep for the fuck of it since they did not use it. I had a great jump kick breaking boards held by one of my students that was sitting on the shoulders of another. That might have been the highest and best kick in my life and they "Threw it out". They also fucked up my nickname given because of Martial Arts, not given by a girl, ...lol remember, it was 'Snake" they freakin put Srvake? WTF? That sounds like a Greek sandwich. Fucking, how do you get SrVake out of "Snake" I had people ask me what nationality I am? after that bullshit. They didn't get it. Neither did I care anymore. I never went to any proms since Jr. High. The closest I came was when I was asked by an Armenian girl, I was friends with to meet her parents and tell them I was taking her to the senior prom. I was to fake them out and then drop her off to meet a black kid, Ron, her parents forbid her to ever see or think about. He was cool and I was glad to. I looked around and not one person was worth sticking around for, so I left. I already made my memories of high school, and some were forced and made for me. It was the end of a long but action-packed adventure. I was asked to sit in the library with some other kids that I guess were in the same boat that I was, not knowing if they made the cut to graduate and walk with the others on stage at graduation. I said it in the beginning, and I will repeat it now. I found out the day I graduated that I passed. No shit.

Chapter Four

"LEGEND OF THE SQUARE BADGE"
THE BIRTH OF A 'BUFF'

1987- So now that I am out of High school, I had thought about what was next. I was not really in a rush to try college full time yet or at all. I discussed it with my parents and told them I wanted to open a school to teach Martial Arts so I didn't have to use other people's Dojos or private homes or ours to learn my Self Defense Program. Of course, because of my track record of irresponsibility and troubles, they shot that idea down and told me to either go to Community college nearby, or work. I was 19 - years old, yeah, don't forget I got left back in 4th grade and needed to do more than just my Kung Fu they said. I stopped the Tae Kwon Do and Goju Ryu Karate to fully focus on just Shaolin Kung Fu and teach on the side whenever I could but that was a very few times I would be called now that everyone is doing their own thing. I posed in the October edition of Inside Kung Fu Magazine with one of my masters back then and thought it would trigger some possible work in acting in action films or something. I tried out for things as they came but nothing "Big" ever came about except instructional videos for select isolated interest groups, like Martial Artists and later would be Military and Law Enforcement types. Will get there later. I did the usual hanging out in town at the Pizza place or in front of the Grand Union or movie theater and see who would show up, any possible parties, or just general fun. One night in the parking lot, I was talking to some high school friends when I overheard some loudmouth threatening one of my friends and pushing him around. He was obviously drunk and slurring every word, but one thing I did to her clearly was his threats to me. He went by 'Mike' and he attended another school, but was familiar with my crowd too. He told me if I didn't shut up that he would take a bat or a pole to my legs and see how good my karate is then. I told him he could go get whatever he wanted, and that he was drunk and stupid and should have someone bring him home. Mike then said he would go home and get a gun and bring it back to shoot me. That was it, and I told him to cut the shit with the talk and come at me anytime he wanted and felt brave enough to. He tried running at me to tackle me only making it necessary to move out of the way and trip him on his big fat dumb ass. He yelled again, "That does it, I am going to get my gun and come back to take care of your ass!". Instead, Mike came back with 3 local Police cars who apparently were sent for me from a drunken BS statement he gave down the street at the Police station. One of the Cops knew me and said I could follow them or hop in the car quickly for a talk. I sat at the station thinking nothing of it. An officer was typing my information as I gave it like basics, name, occupation, address, etc. He stopped after a minute and asked me if I was one of Matty Devine's sons. I said "yes, why?". He rolled his eyes and asked me why I didn't tell him that. I said what the fuck does that have to do with anything, I am not in trouble, and this was a drunk guy threatening me and if anything, I want to press charges for attempted assault. The officer introduced himself and said his father works with my dad at the FBI and that I was being charged with Harassment and he already entered me in the system making a card that gets forwarded to court. I said I wanted to counter charge and went back and forth. He said it's like a traffic ticket violation and gave me an appearance ticket and let me go. I saw Mike the next day and he apologized and said he was only trying to scare me. We had lunch and a laugh over it at Friendly's and then went to the station to drop all charges. Would you believe I had to answer about that dropped charge for about 20 more years with jobs and background checks I had processed for. Some Bullshit can fuck your life up boy.

1988-I decided to take one or two classes at my local Community

College in Criminal Justice. Two reasons were my dad of course being an agent and remembering a demonstration a Police Sergeant gave in Defensive Tactics at my High School on a career day. I took Juvenile Justice and Criminal Investigation to start. Of course, my instructors were from our local town Police Department, so my last name rang a bell with most. I was hooked by the war stories these seasoned instructors gave on cases, the multiple types of crimes and methods out there, the works. I also remember being impressed with a K-9 demonstration on that same day as the defensive tactics demo. So that was now going to be my goal, and once again fingers in a lot of bowls can become one bowl I thought. I wanted to be a K-9 Cop who taught defensive tactics. So, all my interests of Martial Arts, K9 (Shepherds) and Police work would all be wrapped up in one career, at the same time, one place. I started where most do, being under 21, at working security jobs to get some experience under my belt and develop a resume. This and attending a class or two a week were also helping my relationship and talks with my dad who started opening to me about cases he was allowed to talk about, methods or techniques he would use for interviewing and or interrogations. I think I joked before, but I do believe he had the best practice of these skills by having 6 of us kids to use them on. One title helped the other, and I now know that as a father myself of 3 boys of my own. What I did lack, was the patience, and understanding of rights, teamwork, and law all together of the do(s) and don'ts yet. That would take play real soon in a bunch of crap I pulled. I may have been taught a lot, or told a lot about, but did not follow the rules when I saw things happen in front of me. Like everything before this, I had to learn the hard way. So, get ready, this is No Shit!

I got a few Security jobs. Some shifts were the same day back-to-back, some with different companies, some only once or twice a week or on call. Of course, the first place I wanted to do security at was the mall. I was still kind of a mall rat anyway and knew most of the people who hung out there. I thought it would be a win/win by making it seem like I could be a big influence to others to leave if complained about. Mostly for loitering or blocking doorways, going in and out with no purpose. If they saw me as the one telling them, I thought they would respect me more and listen to me more than they would any other guard. Well, not the result at all! I was too familiar and friendly with them, to the point they felt comfortable calling me rent a cop, square badge patrol, Smokey the Bear Hat, Mall Cop.. etc. I told them that it is affecting my job, and to go out in their cars, hang across the mall at the movie theater lot and filter back little by little but only if they are going to play and spend money at the arcade and not sit on the floor or keep running around, echoing their noise throughout the mall. That seemed to work for a bit, but eventually there were those I did not know too well. One, claimed to be a Golden Gloves Boxer, and told me to Fuck Off when I told him to move along when he and some others were smoking between the two sets of exit doors, instead of outside. I asked him why he would narrate his life and fighting resume when talking to me. He said he heard about me from some "Friends" in common and that he would like to 'Spar' sometime. I told him of course I was not interested, but maybe he could teach me boxing one day if he had the time and wanted to hang. Confused and hesitant, he just shrugged and said "whatever" and left. I may have catered to his ego, to de-escalate his challenge talk, but I really was interested in learning real boxing. It was always kind of semi taught in Martial Arts as far as hand position, but not in the footwork, and dodge head maneuvers I could have used in school when fighting, and not have my face being used to block jabs.

Just like in High School, I still had my 'Shadows'. The ones that would hang with me whenever or wherever they could like they were attached by the hip. During school years, it was R. Angelo, and now that I was out of school, it started with another one, that was Paul. I called him Paulie like from 'Rocky'. Paulie was at the mall every day in and out and never stopped walking everywhere in between until I got off or had a break. We would hang there, or at his house in West Nyack NY, where sometimes his sister, Dawn, I knew before him and went to school with would join us. Paulie had what later I was told was a Biochemical Imbalance or Bipolar. He would have tangents and go off about things but always yell in mid air to the side and never make eye contact like he is telling a story to furniture or something. I tried teaching him about mannerisms and some Martial Arts, because he had the interest and body frame for vigorous workouts. I introduced the idea of him bouncing with me at a local club that I offered to teach the staff at. The manager, 'Frankie', asked Paulie if he could do what (I just demonstrated) as good as me. I guided Paulie with some scenarios I know I went over a thousand times with, but he was not as fast or effective as I had hoped he would be. I also tried getting him a Security job at the mall, but they recognized him as one of the 'Loiterers' that they see in and out and that he was too young and immature and didn't look the part. Paulie kept long hair and looked like a wet rat most of the time. Hate to say it, but they were right. One guard, a "Time to make the Donuts" fat ass cop mustached loudmouth, told me after my inquiry about Paulie, that if he saw Paulie hanging around again, he was going to arrest his ass for trespassing and anything else he could make up. I was furious and told this piece of crap off and said that Paulie, being like a little brother to me, will not be touched by anybody, and that I am his ride home and he cannot go home because of situations he would not understand and that I take full responsibility for him. I said, "You have all the seniors walking around the mall with no purpose of shopping but to just do laps, and you have your own little slut cakes. I see you flirting with hanging around the booth you never leave because you are afraid to show your fat ass!" So Paulie is not an issue unless you make him one, so Shut the Fuck Up! you have no powers to arrest anyone!". That did not go over too well, so of course little baby bubba fat ass dimed me out to the supervisor who told me I was on a probationary period, still new, and they could fire me for insubordination. I told them in response that I knew my rights and Paulie's, that I study Criminal Justice, and know a lot about the law and behavior (Due to my dad's lessons and stories), and that Paulie will not be a problem, and neither will I be one, but I will not tolerate threats of any kind and that I am very productive. Now, as I said, I had a lot going on at the same time, burning the candle and frankly the whole bed at all ends. A few Security gigs, bouncing on call at a teen club, teaching whoever and wherever I could, and still trying to have fun times in between.

One of my security/door man gigs was at the movie theater across the street from the mall, but not with the same company as the mall had a contract with and in just plain black dress clothes. Like a glorified usher with a few hats to wear. One night, two guys were outside the theater doors but close enough to the entrance to be heard and in the way of people going in and out. They appeared intoxicated and were cursing out loud making fun of or making general contact verbally harassing patrons of the theater. Asking people if "They liked the Fucking Movie" and "Don't you think this place sucks", or personal questions to any females like "You have a boyfriend with you?" etc. I went outside and let them know that I would call the police if they didn't have any purpose there and that they were disrupting business and patrons. They laughed at me and asked, "Who the fuck are you?" and said, "We have every right to be here" and "it's a free country" and all that. It was a battle of who knew what rights, and testosterone challenge. One of them said he finally had enough of the bullshit and took a beer out of his pocket. I guess he had hidden to sneak into the theater with, if they were coming in at all. I told him they are not coming in, and to empty the beer or go away. He got close enough to where his next "Fuck You", spat all over me, beer and saliva and stink mixed. That was it!

I took him by his poking hand. He touched me while pointing his finger in my chest while he spat those last words and attempted to arm bar him with the wrist lock first, when his friend tried interfering, but I kicked him back. His buddy started telling me how he is a law student, and I cannot do this, or that and have no right to detain or physically restrain his friend and blah blah blah. I told him I have a right not to be spit on, cursed at, or touched in any way and that he would be next if he didn't back off and shut up. Just then, a Police car pulls to the curb, and a quick 'blooop' from the siren PA system echoed for the altercation to stop obviously. Two older gentlemen got out, but although it was my town's Police car markings, these guys were in dark navy-blue uniforms top and bottom like NYPD wore, and no weapon was visible on their duty belt except a flashlight, PR 24 baton, and cuffs. One had an accent, a little guy, who looked like a Mario Brother from a game, and the other looked like a mix of Joe Piscopo and Richard Simmons with gray afro-hair. The one with the accent had told me to back off and asked what was going on? Of course, the loudmouth drunk fucktard tried answering, until I once again told him to shut the fuck up and let me speak. I gave a short, detailed brief like I was on 'Dragnet' giving just the facts and asked them what they can do? They told the guys to dump their beers over in the grass and take off or go eat somewhere to blow off steam. I waited until they were done watching the asswipes leave and stopped them before they went into the patrol car to ask the obvious question. "Who, What, Where and How etc.." of doing what they are doing. They were part of the Police department's Auxiliary Police. I never heard of it but the one with the accent, told me they do traffic duty, attend games for appearance of security or lot detail, any event, parade, and "We patrol as the eyes and ears for the regular department." I said to myself, "Self" I must join this if I am going to reach my goal of being a Cop or something when I am of age and accepted. I asked if they get paid, and he said no. Just tell people you are "Part Time" when they ask why there is a difference in uniform. The other Auxiliary guy was quick to get back in the Police car and hint they had to go. I asked if they had a card or something, and they told me just to inquire with the chief of police. (Challenge Accepted!)

As soon as I could, I asked my father if he knew about this division of Police called the Auxiliary Police. He asked me why, so of course I told him what happened and that they said I could join. He reminded me about the time I snuck to New York City and met some Guardian Angels because they were at or visiting someone competing at the Karate tournament I went to. He reminded me of who they were in his opinion and said the same thing about the Auxiliary, but more as a vague warning, not exactly as a turn down. He said some people join to have an excuse to have some false sense of authority over people and end up in trouble or hurting someone or get in trouble by interfering with the real Police doing their job. My father warned me that not all Police respect the Auxiliary and think they are a bunch of 'Buffs' Wannabe cops' that couldn't make it onto the real force. He said he knows a lot of cops that are real Police officers that don't belong on the force, never mind the Auxiliary. Like this one douchebag Cop, who set himself out to see my dad and make conversation with him on the road, outside church, or at the deli. My father always talked shit after they would come across each other. Pointing out how this Cop would have his hand or arm resting on his weapon (Like a hog leg) while talking or bringing up cases with shop talk to be significant in some way to my dad. I asked if it would be ok to join if it gave me experience and network in the department to possibly join a regular force when I was old enough to. My father said if that's what I wanted to do, then I should start taking Police exams in multiple cities and eventually get picked up somewhere but do not ignore my studies. As usual, he harped on education because, as he would say "it's getting tougher, and more qualifications needed now compared to my day". I went to the next scheduled meeting of the Auxiliary Police after the Chief of Police told me when it was and that there was going to be some changes soon of who is going to be the liaison, and a new chief announced eventually I would be talking with. I was given a few shirts, and pants and some traffic control stuff like a flashlight with an orange cone, traffic reflective vest, gloves, etc, and a hat. No badge yet or ID was ready. The meeting itself was about upcoming events, introductions of newbies like me and a go around of who is available for what that month as far as patrol hours and attending/working the events. I volunteered for what I could, especially patrol after checking my schedule with my multiple gigs. I didn't want to quit my paying jobs for volunteer stuff but even if it meant staying up and doing it the same day there was an event, I was there. A short time after joining the Auxiliary, I had received my Police Department ID with a big black stamp across the middle that said AUXILIARY but still no badge yet. One day I wanted to "Flex my new authority" around like I was a legend (in my own mind.) I went and did some day patrol on my own in my own car and decided to visit my old High School and show off my "New "Position". I still had friends in lower grades who were seniors by this time and knew when they were on lunch and where they hung out. I walked in with my chest puffed proud in my new garb and went straight to the principal's office to do the same Bullshit that cop does to my dad, like "Look at Me" The big Deal". He sat me down after looking me over and asked confusingly in tone, "What are you doing here?", I told him "Patrol of course" and he said "Well, I am busy so good seeing you, but he has to go, so off you go" He looked me more closely and I could see his mouth move. Now, remember, I didn't get issued a badge yet from the Police department for Auxiliary, but guess what my cheesedick wannabe ass did? I wore my duplicate Police shaped security one with badge number and I could see him trying to memorize it. I went to the back of the school where some friends were and they were checking out my personal self-Buffed out Police equipped car and asking some stuff, when all of sudden, the Principal comes out and tells all to get back inside and walked briskly by me telling me "Terry, The Chief wants to talk to you as soon as you can", then he walked to the wall that most hang out at to tell them it's time to go in. I looked at him and remember that he was always by the book and how the fuck could I forget that? Now, being the narcissistic buff I was, I had my mall security white shirt inside my bag with my real security square badge. That clearly stated "Security". I went to the Police Department and asked to see the chief, and he said he was expecting me. I was let in and sat down feeling that hot fizzy dizziness, nausea of getting caught or in trouble type of feeling. The chief smiled and said he got a call from the High School Principal, and that he gave him my badge number and everything, while pointing at my chest. I looked at the chief and said with a chuckle, "I don't have a badge yet, this is my security badge from the mall that I told him I was on my way to, and that I am going to patrol shift there." "The principal must be confused of what I meant sir, because I mentioned joining here when he asked what I have been up to, so I guess I talked too fast or mentioned it back-to-back like it was one in the same." The chief grinned with a half ass smile mixed with puss on his face and went into his drawer and threw me an Auxiliary Police Badge. Whew! No Shit! But wait. There is more. A whole lot more to come.

I was not only good at covering my ass, fast thinking (Lying), and pretending, but that also included impersonations. As in, voices. Any TV, movie, or live character, when heard enough and practiced a little, I could imitate just about anyone's voice and character. I still worked a few different security gigs at the same time for different companies, like I said earlier. I didn't know there was any clause with the mall security contract, that we were not allowed to work for any other security company. I came from one job and was seen wearing that shirt with a different logo, before changing at the mall for my scheduled shift I was almost late for. The female security officer who has been there a while told me that the supervisor wanted to see me in his office in the back where the mall manager area is. I walked in and gave the greeting of the day to the supervisor, and he looked up at the female guard who used the radio in her hand to point the antenna like a finger at me and nod like "Here he is sir" yup yup "I fetched him for ya". This is when I realized that she is the one who saw me wearing a different shirt and dimed me out like a snake in the grass. What the fuck? The supervisor told me of the rules and said he cannot have me working for multiple companies or at least not wear their shirt inside this contracted account area. I told him I understood, but reminded him he has actual cops working security for him (Moonlighting) and that is against both his and their regulations, and that some also bounce at bars, etc. He told me to forget about the extra work if it does not show up here, and I do not let it interfere with my shift by being late or calling off. I went home after shift and wrote a whole statement of everything I knew that each of the other guards did on the side. I knew this female didn't like me, because someone she was with, whether it was a husband or boyfriend was a cop, that brought her as a guest at the Shields Meeting my father started bringing me to if it was award night or a special dinner to start networking in Law Enforcement. I went to greet her at one she showed at, and she looked away rolling her eyes while I tried to shake her hand in surprise to see her there. She was just as surprised also and made it clear she had zero interest in knowing me. I always caught her whispering while looking at me to whoever was in the security booth in the middle of the mall. I saw her once or twice after years of real experience, so the atmosphere was better with mutual respect when she found out what you will read about my career later. The next day after that "Talking to" by the supervisor, I guess he wanted to make sure I understood, by calling my house looking to speak to my father, because I guess they knew each other from events in Law Enforcement foundations like the Shields member dinners I mentioned. This hump had the nerve to call my house? well guess what? Challenge accepted. I recognized his voice immediately and went full Mr. Devine (my dad) voice and character on his ass. He started with trying to remind me (As my father) how he knew me and reminders of cases, bla bla bla!..they discussed. I figured he was a retired cop. Anyway, he went on to say how "Terry is obsessed with going after shoplifters, going after loiterers, he is wearing other companies' clothes to work, telling off my other guards, blah blah bla. I (As my father) told this guy that

"Terry has a lot of knowledge from me teaching him about crimes, behavior, law, and doing what's right. Terry studies Criminal Justice in college and works back-to-back to afford things so we don't have to pay for them. Terry told me everything that your guards have said to him, including arresting his friends? ratting him out for putting them in their place after insulting him and he defends himself? Have you spelled out exact work demands and expectations to Terry about his job description and its limitations? Are you not supposed to apprehend shoplifters when Security is called? I would appreciate you discussing this with Terry in a one-on-one meeting face to face with a clear training plan if not already so there is no misunderstanding or lawsuit by you not covering your bases giving these guards the notion, they are free to do what cops do. Understand?"

He said "Yes, I do, and did not know Terry was that passionate about the job, and his background" I will definitely have a sit down and make sure all resources are available to him to excel and be successful". "I am sorry to bother with this" and I will see you at the next Shields or Knights of Columbus Matty".. I then finished the call with..." Yeah ok der"..like there, but that's how he (My dad) said it, like it was with a ('D') Dis, Dat, and a few of Dose too...lol. My father was a genius agent, mathematician, and my mother said he had other Master scholar type recognition in the arts but still had that NY street pronunciation of certain words.

Mission accomplished, I went to work the next shift scheduled and the supervisor stayed on duty to have our one on one and friendly conversation about 'My Dad' and how things are to be fully communicated for now on. Not too long after that situation, when I was settled in and in good standing, a new management and contract came for security for the mall, and I was allowed to be transferred right over. It also brought about a new supervisor and out went

'My father's buddy'..lol. This guy, not remembering his name, was definitely a retired cop, possibly NYPD or corrections. Typical cop mustache, Captain Kangaroo posture body and hair line rim. I will just call him Bob, like the Practice 'Hitting Dummy' in Martial Arts. Bob did not like anything I did. If I had given the greeting of the day to the mall manager, he would shush me while walking with me and act like we are peasants not allowed to talk to the higher up echelon. On one occasion, I had an apprehension of a lifter who took over $500 of goods. I had the written statement of witnesses and video showing clear evidence of his shoplifting. I started paperwork on him for our records until the Police arrived to process and take a report from us. Bob calls for me to go do some trivial tasks with maintenance or something regarding a door staying open, that other guards outside in the halls could have done. I radioed him back letting him know my status with a lifter and awaiting Police to arrive. Bob, on the radio and out loud yells at me saying "Will you stop with all that nonsense" and get over to maintenance. I was pissed off enough having this fucktard speak like that on the radio, but to do it in full earshot of the criminal in my mind was unforgivable as much as it was embarrassing. I told him I was in front of the subject and to cease radio communication and come straight to the office to take over watching the subject unless he wanted to let him go and explain to the arriving officers why. Police arrived shortly after and took him with all I had given them for evidence. I told Bob later, he could call the department and ask for all we had on the subject because I had to go to maintenance on his orders and did not have time to make copies for our records and handed it all over to the Police. Bob one day said he was going on leave or going somewhere for a while. A down to earth young security officer who knew some Ninja shit, and was looking into corrections as career confided in me by stating that while I was off, the Mall Manager asked Bob who would be in charge as acting supervisor while he was gone? When the contract account manager for security suggested I would be a good choice, this young guard told me Bob said out loud and clear in front of all, "Over my Dead Body will Terry ever be in charge." I confronted Bob immediately the next time I saw him, and he turned as red as a fire hydrant and said it was not personal, but it is because of lack of experience as a supervisor that he meant that. I told him that from what I saw, it didn't take much but kissing ass to the mall manager, carrying a radio and wearing a polyester blazer acting busy by pacing around the mall and drinking coffee. I did more as a guard than he did as a supervisor. But...as I reflect back..I am glad he didn't leave me in charge, because after being retired myself now, fuck that!..Who wants it? Extra headache and responsibility for a dollar or two more an hour? Keep that shit. But, as a Buff back then, it was a resume builder to say I was a supervisor of security. That title and more came many times over in the future, I may not have deserved any position back then, but all is not lost because of that square badge patrol shit.

I stayed on that mall contract for a little while longer, while at the same time increasing my presence with the Auxiliary and offering more shifts or detail help. I left the movie theater job, and really was not teaching much. I was still hanging with a lot of the mall gang, and shared some good times with them, but unfortunately some bad times too. One girl I knew, very quiet and sweet, had an asshole brother who I would catch regularly pinning either his own sister or some female he was with against a wall with his finger in their face while telling them off or threatening something. The guy never let up and it was like Groundhog Day, until one time it would change forever. At the arcade we hung at, down from the mall, this guy was yelling at his sister as usual, but something was upsetting her more this time to the point she ran out onto the main road. Some days, these kids had drag races up and down this route, no matter how much they had been warned. If timing could not have sucked enough, the girl did not even make it to the median in the middle of the road while running from her brother, before one of these assholes revved his car even louder and plowed her into the air, cartwheeling until a final drop on her head, killing her instantly. I went to the wake and funeral, and to the final plot resting grounds, said my prayers with a tear, but I could tell that I was looked at as an outsider, wannabe cop or friend to these misfits. Especially her brother who felt guilty for what he felt caused her to run and didn't want any reminder of "Being a bad guy" by seeing me with a judging eye. I know this to be true, because after the incident, I asked the investigating detective if I could help him on the scene. He knew my family and that I was an Auxiliary. I told him all I knew, including how there seemed to be no attempt by the driver to stop or slow down at all. That was verified by the lack of friction marks showing any attempt to brake until after the impact happened. I guess he really wanted to win that race. Someone confided in me and told me the overall resentment they had of me investigating the scene. I could not let her lay in vain. Sorry, but she deserved better. It's all Kung Fu. The decisions you make, the voice you listen to, and the path you decide to take. I chose the path of the Blue Line, that I still did not fully understand, and would not for some time after.

I quit my mall security job shortly after I ran into my Kung Fu masters, who were shopping there and kind of laughed at me wearing the 'Smokey the Bear' hat issued and such. They said they thought I was a real cop, and what I was doing there, and so on and so on. I told them everything was part time, and I had my fingers in a lot of bowls but would be around the studio more after leaving at least one of the jobs and put more attention into my Martial Arts and stay in their favor. After all, they did a lot for me and let me be part of their successful media, and kind of their poster boy for the Kung Fu Center. At least in the beginning. The Kung Fu center had a good number of students in a short time. Just like in school, you had your different personalities. You had 100% energy, all in, motivated guys like me, then you had the ones who made everything look like it was killing them, with the big puss strain pain face with every move or exercise and sweat like a hostage doing it. The ones you don't not want are the bad hygiene nasty students to even look at never mind working out with or must get physical with drills. There was one, who ``If wiping your ass had a face" looked like and smelled like every single time he attended. Greasy hair, untucked filthy shirt that looked like what I just said, about wiping an ass with, and crud filled long fingernails. He would sneeze then blow his nose into his hand and wipe on his pants instead of excusing himself to get cleaned up or a t least a tissue. I had enough, and told Sifu, that hygiene is everybody's business since it affects us all and our health. I said it was dangerous if we get scratched by the guy accidently or not, if any bacteria causing staff or worse, MRSA is caused by him simply not washing himself, cutting his nails, or cleaning his clothing before attending class. They had a talk with him, but it went nowhere, until he did. Thank God. The other kind of student, that you find everywhere, is the real holistic deep meditator, that must fold his legs, connect his fingers together and flip his eyes back into a trance, and you would just be expecting to let out a big OMMMM!! And see him levitate..lol. He is the kind that thinks we are still in 2500 BC Shaolin temple days and walks like he doesn't want to rip rice paper and give slow silent eye flutter bows after every word the Sifu said. Now, the rest I would categorize as the Power Stompers, that act like a lightning bolt will be generated and thrown from their hands with every move in a form. They think by being louder and stomping into every move and turn, equates to more effective technique. Like me, there were a few experienced martial Artists from different disciplines like Mantis, Kung Fu, Wushu, or Karate and other styles. My buddy Tom I mentioned earlier came a few times to check out the class. One well known instructor, who's female student did the instructional video with me, decided to fuck with me when he found out I taught on the side and asked where I got my ranks in Karate and Tae Kwon Do from and any other school I have been to. He made up a story of visiting one of my former masters from childhood, saying he was inviting him to attend a demonstration or something and claimed the Master never heard of me. Then like "Dance Monkey Dance! "he demanded I do a Black Belt form for him right there and then. I decided to do KORYO from Tae Kwon Do, but know I fucked up one of the moves that was similar in Goju Ryu with certain hand movements with a double arm maneuver or something. He just nodded, wiping his nose like he proved a point. I looked around for approval and support of those that knew my background and qualifications were beyond reproach. I told this chicken fucker that I have been a Martial Artist since grade school, and I don't need to answer to him or anyone. He said "I will pay you, you teach me your self-defense" like chopped caveman talk. I told him I do not have my own school, and it's a program and I would be glad to show him anytime, and forms are not part of it or should be relied on, because I have not had to perform them for a while at that point. My buddy pointed out that maybe I knew too many and it was easy to get confused with many styles at the same time, but if I could show 8 different forms without my fat ass sticking out losing balance, then I would get credit in that instructor's eyes. I don't dance on command, especially if you are not my instructor and fuck him with his lying ass. It bothered me to no end, so I called my former master and right away he greeted me like I never left and asked how things were, and how the family was etc. I inquired if anyone was around from the Kung Fu center talking about me or a demonstration. He said no, not at all. Fucking liar, I knew it. That asswipe in class was trying to bait me. I guess because I was the golden boy, the first student there, and he was not getting all the attention he obviously starved for 24/7. His female student told me "He is just like that, an ego maniac that has to be the best one around and be recognized, and don't worry about him" she said she was tired of his shit too and that they were not an item, like I thought they were. Would have gone further with that but didn't want any more drama. I thought all would blow over, but now some of the students that came occasionally, would be wiseasses and greet me by a few titles with a stutter like they were confused what to call me. It was like "Hey ..Sifu..Sens. I.. I mean Sabu..officer..master..". I told them that I hold only one title in that class, and that was my name. Fuck titles, put up or shut up. I told this story and situation to my group of students I would meet up with. Some from High school and others from hanging around town or neighborhood. We would use my yard, or one of theirs if not their downstairs. My friend Paulie would not stop laughing and repeating the stutter multi title greeting I told him the students were jokingly using on me. He wouldn't stop repeating it and following it with that Arnold Horseshack from 'Welcome Back Kotter' donkey laugh. I just aged myself there. I yelled at him, forgetting he had "issues". We walked like we always did from one side of town to the other and to this day I do not remember what triggered an argument, but it ended with me having to smack him to calm him down and not be aggressive toward me outside of the Diner we went to. I heard a rumor later in time, he was arrested for taking someone's rowboat out for a joyride from their property, and was put in a psychiatric facility, when they had them opened at least.

So now my life was just Kung Fu, hanging with friends, a class once or twice a week, and the Auxiliary. I needed some paying job though. I went back to the mall, but to the attached Sears department store and applied to the Loss prevention section to be a plain clothes security guy. A Huey Lewis looking guy, stepped out and took my resume with him outside and told me to follow. He started smoking and after a big smokey exhale, told me my resume was very impressive and told me that we had multiple functions as a Loss Prevention ``Agent". It was more than catching shoplifters on camera or running out the store. It was looking for patterns of revenue loss, watching the cashiers exchange, picking up drawers when they reached certain tolls and switching often. It was holding meetings of safety and crime prevention and a watch program involving all tenants and vendors. I was interested of course in mostly just apprehending thieves and not having to wear a uniform. Also, we got a huge discount on great clothes as an employee on top of the sale prices...yes!. Being the new guy, I was expected to be there to open, and help any vendor due to come in to deliver goods and assure it was written down if no manifest was given. I was introduced to a young guy, who was there a little longer than me. He told me about who is who, and what to look out for including what employees were nice and which were a problem. He had his fiancé at the time, (I say that word "Had", for a reason,) come by for lunch sometimes. Beautiful Indian girl that looked like a thicker Priyanka Chopra, in a good way. I will mention her again later in a different scenario. We had good cooperation from most, especially the head of the electronics area who has been there for years. Everything from lights to refrigerators to TVs, you name it. He came in early and always stopped by our office where we had camera screens fill up the wall seeing every angle in the store and ability to follow or zoom the same. One morning, that manager was in our office before I even went in, and he told me to look at the screen showing the men's department. I couldn't believe my eyes when I saw that same young partner of mine, who showed me the ropes and who is who and who to look out for, STEALING CLOTHES and shoving them away in whatever he could. He had no clue the manager was in already, camera screens on, and I would be there early too. So, my first apprehension would be one of our own. Decisions...my friends, 'it's all Kung Fu.' I got into a few spats with customers who would think I was hanging around them or watching, probably true. One I had it out with, left his kid, a toddler alone for a long time to wander around far away enough you would wonder where the parents are. Anything could have happened. When I saw this on camera, I hit the floor to watch even longer, the ignorance and self-centered behavior of the parent not paying attention or caring where their child is. I finally decided to go talk to the child until the father made an appearance. He had the balls to say to me "Yeah, I saw you looking at me like I was going to steal something", I got a fucking receipt, or something to that nature. I told him it was about his child walking around far away aimlessly and him not having a clue where he was, or the dangers of what he would try to lift or play with, or just get picked up possibly all together. That argument got loud, and my boss said my body language on camera looked too violent and aggressive, but he could not determine if it warranted being fired because there was no audio, and he believed my concern for the child's welfare was genuine. Well, that was one mess cleaned up, but as I say, it's all about decisions. These next ones were not exactly good ones.

Chapter Five

"WOMANIZER!"
'CALL ME DICK...TRACY'

I started to get to know all the vendors in the store, and who was who, and who to watch out for and who I could rely on for any assistance or help. One guy, who worked in the stereo department, was a bartender and member of the AOH (Ancient order of Hibernians) an Irish Organization that, just like the VFW or Knights of Columbus, have their own chapters and programs, fundraisers, political involvement dealing with Irish issues or members. I went as an excuse to drink on a Tuesday night and met a lead bagpiper who I took lessons from once a week. I could never read music and cheated at what I did know. So, until I learned enough, I would march holding the American or Ireland flag during St. Patrick's Day Parades for them.

Just like anyplace else, I also knew what departments the most attractive women had working in them. I would set myself out to pass by and "Check in " on a few of them daily but not hang too long, since I was not supposed to be an obvious employee at all. There was one girl in the electronics area that would stop everything she was doing, whether it was talking to a customer, coworker or eating just to look at me and smile with a wave. Eventually it was followed by a finger wave gesture to come to her to talk. I would spend a few minutes to ask the usual cheesedick stuff like her name, how long has she worked there? when does she get a break? and do you want to...never mind. She was Peruvian or Guatemalan, I forget which and had that Selma Hayek type accent with a raspy tone. I convinced her to have dinner one night at a Mexican restaurant only minutes away. It was a nice setting and all we did was stare at each other and caressing each other's thighs under the table in between some unprovoked laughs for no reason. I asked her if she was born here in the states and she said no that her and 'HER HUSBAND,' were not from here. (Sound of brakes slamming in my head..EEERRRPP!) Well, obviously the next question was, "who is your husband? and where is he now?" She told me the whole sob story about how angry and abusive he is all the time, and that he was the little guy I pass by every day when I do a round, and that he works in a different department but in the straight eyeline of her right down an aisle directly across from her. Which to me, means he has seen me flirting with her and knows where she is now. I walked her to the car, had some finger fun time like she was a new bowling bowl and then dropped her off at her car in a lot we met at. After a week or two after that adventure, and seeing her husband give me the death stare on the daily, I was called to my office and met up with the electronics manager who was rewinding some footage on the screen showing his area. There was little Ms. Muffet who I poked in the Tuffet, stealing money from the register one time, taking a card from someone and sliding it thru her own device under the counter, to steal debit information and returning it to the customer, and bringing it to her husband in the middle of an aisle to pass off. This kind of fraud was above my paygrade so my boss, and this manager took care of the processing. It could have gotten ugly if I was used and went further with this trick, and to tell you the truth, that was her plan I bet the whole time.

I didn't stop there, although you would think I should have, but there was a variety of different cultures and beauty in this one store, and I was young and single. At that time anyway, but soon to change. I had started dating a Dominican girl who worked there but I forgot what department. Just when I thought all was going well enough to the point, I wanted to be exclusive, she dropped the "let's be friends" bomb on me, saying she didn't have that desire to continue anymore. I was not used to being rejected, maybe because it really didn't happen in an actual relationship that was more than a title for the first time. I didn't understand why I was so upset and heartbroken and starting whimpering in voice, almost begging her to reconsider and she clearly again nodded and sighed with an I am sorry but no, this is how I feel, I don't want to continue being with you and I do not know why, I just don't like you like that. I told her that this "Happened to be a coincidence" that she made this decision after I just met her family at her house days earlier. Maybe they didn't want her with a white boy, a cop, or wannabe cop? I don't know, but yeah, a thousand thoughts went through my mind in denial that it could have been just me or feelings fading. Well, there is a saying," If you want to get over someone, get under another". While working at the mall, I got my first credit card. I was happier than a pig in shit. I used it at Sears with my discount, I used it at the leather shop for a total Guido long leather jacket that went down to my calves and bought drinks for my brothers and his friends at a club I was able to get into since I did lip sync contests there. I didn't think there was a limit on an American Express. Well, I proved that theory wrong. I went out to a club in NJ a friend of mine had VIP status with. It was a mixture of dance sections, and different music on each level. I was headed to the bathroom, and suddenly, I got pulled back by my arm, turning me hard enough to almost stumble and fall onto the one holding me. It was the Indian fiancé (Priyanka lookalike) who made it clear right away that she was the FORMER fiancé to the asshole I worked with that turned out to be a thief. She said all was trashed after that. This particular room we were talking in had black lights throughout the whole section and I could see she was wearing colored contacts, but it was still attractive enough to stare at. She had evidently been there a while drinking and was all over the place. She finally decided to sit on my lap and "Dance". She was wearing a very sheer white mini dress with maybe a thong if anything, but you could not see any evidence of that. She went full exorcist on me with the head lashing and rocking like nobody else was around. I told her we should get out of there and take it somewhere else. She stopped everything, turned to me and took my fingers on my right hand and went down on them like I had the last bit of icing left over in a bowl on them, and she wanted it all. She straddled me, and I may as well have paid for a VIP room in a strip club. I will leave the rest and ending, a happy one, to your imagination. And.... Breathe!

The last adventure I had in this job, I say last because it got me fired, was when I was off duty but wanted to shop and flirt with some girls from the fashion and cosmetics area. Go figure. I went and hung out at their register, and it was close to closing time but many customers were left and the girls were complaining about how long they were going to have to stay and clean up after these people. For whatever stupid reason, thinking with the wrong head most likely, I picked up the desk phone and punched in the code for the PA system speaker and let out a big, long announcement that kind of went like this: "Attention Sears Shoppers, the store is now closing, so please immediately make your way to the registers or out the exits if you have not purchased any items." The head manager of Sears stormed out of his office and passed by me, but doubled back and asked if I Heard that announcement, and who did it? I denied knowing who did it because I didn't want the girls to be accused of convincing me to help close early and I would tell him when we were out of their area. Too late. My boss came the next day to me and told me that I was terminated for everything from start to finish. The arguments with customers, the hanging out with staff, obvious relationships beyond professional with one or two, and now the denial of making the announcement. I tried to explain, but he interrupted and said he was a retired Lieutenant in the NYPD, and didn't try to even begin to bullshit him. So, I didn't. I told him I was helping the girls close early but didn't want him to think they pushed me into it. He said not to worry, that this was all on me. See Ya!

I didn't go long without work and continued to patrol the county with the Auxiliary. One regular partner was the one that I met that night at the movie theater that rushed his partner to leave. We had good conversations about who has what reputation, good and bad, past events or members that stood out, and the usual jargon to make the shift go by and be interesting. He knew all the hotspots of where he and his regular partner flirted with girls. It is amazing how attracted women are to a uniform, even a volunteer one. One area was of course food courts. It was a great excuse to be there, and many were taking advantage of good weather, staying to talk, and "Observe" the public. I set myself out to get partnered up with either of these two original guys, but sometimes I ended up with one of the Sergeants who had a whole different style and routine as you could imagine. Now, what I am about to tell you, is a NO SHIT moment. One day while patrolling with one of the cool guys, lol we drove in the Grand Union parking lot circling by the theater that I hung out at with friends. I saw some kid doing some shadow boxing and kicking with his friends fooling around. I called out to him and asked where he studies Martial Arts. He told me he was studying NINJITSU UNDER ALEX, that Russian kid that challenged me to that Ninja Death Match he lost badly to. I immediately hid my nameplate by raising my arm to hold my chin like I was intrigued. He said he was training to eventually go against a guy named TERRY DEVINE. (ME!)..NO SHIT!. I turned to my partner and smiled but had to shush him quickly when he confusingly started to tell this kid who I was. The kid caught the idea that maybe we at least knew who he was talking about, and he asked, "why? Do you know him?" ... I humored him and said yeah, I heard he is good and you better practice for a long time before trying because he still is active and never stops learning or teaching. He asked me how I know him so well? that is when I revealed that I was Terry, and to tell Alex the same thing I told him that day I beat him down." You all can work out and practice for 20 years while I sit on my ass, and you will still Never Ever beat me. I won't arrest you for any premeditated plans, but I will leave you spewing in your own juices if you try." The kid was now shaking with nerves and adrenaline kicking, not knowing what to say or do and tried asking me what the deal was between me and Alex like suddenly, we are drinking buddies.? I told him "Unless I wake up with you in the morning, and you have a picture of me in your wallet or I do of you, it's none of your business." He went away with his head down urging his friends to leave with him, into the pizzeria to obviously talk shit about what just happened. Now, back to Women'. A girl came out of the clothing store that was right next to the movie theater where I was having my "Conversation" with the young Ninja apprentice. She had on a simple but complimenting white one-piece pull-down stretch type dress, clinging to her tan gleaming skin like her whole body was waxed and buff shined. She caught me looking, (Most likely drooling) and smiled and asked me if I was really who I said I was or was I trying to scare the kid. I said "Both". She told me she thought it was hilarious like it was a script. This girl was way out of my league. I knew it and eventually, she knew it too, at least in her own mind. I told her I had to go but would love to see her again outside of work and gave her one of my left-over cards I had made for teaching Self Defense. She was impressed, or so she said by saying, "Wow, you just do it all don't you?" Of course, I had to reply with a cheesy, "call me and find out" She gave a squint of her eyes and a gentle smile while turning her head to roll her eyes like "OMG", so I laughed acknowledging my cliché line. Her name was Lisa. We met up for lunch, walked through Paramus mall where she loved shopping for shoes and a black dress like the one I met her in, and said how pretty it was. I, as a man, still do not understand how a simple Black piece of clothing could be called "Pretty" and I think I said that out loud too. I could tell this girl is used to and catered to getting what she wants. She was very independent, but eventually, I broke through that front of being a strong "I don't need anyone's exterior" and had her cuddling and snuggling me every chance she could get. Even while walking hand in hand, she was clingy, or after "Love sessions" but not clingy in a bad way like the 'Witch of School years past' that I never touched or wanted to. I started to feel that wanting more wave, to be exclusive, and it scared me. I started dodging her by putting in more shifts or volunteering for more events with the Auxiliary, and I took a job at Bradlees department store to work loss prevention there. It was right down a few blocks from the Police station so I could do back-to-back work if need be. In the same parking lot of Bradlees, there was a McDonalds that I used to work at when they allowed 15- and 16-year old's to. I in fact taught Karate to the manager there who was so overweight and desperate, he would wear a bodysuit, like stockings under his clothes. I did all I could with advice, routines, nutrition advice, but he eventually started canceling more and more saying he had worked doubles or any excuse not to continue. It was good cash teaching privately. Like running a lemonade stand on a corner. Easy no tax money for something that came simple to me. Nobody thought about liability, contracts, etc. back then. You paid, you went, sweated, beat yourself or someone else up, and went home. Anyway, I saw him on my breaks from Bradlees when I would go there for lunch sometimes and said hello.

While fooling around with the cameras in the office and shifting left and right up and down on a few, I caught a glimpse of a cute girl with dark outlined eyes that I could not tell if it was makeup, or her lashes. I followed her with the cameras (For Training Purposes only...lol) for about a half hour until I decided I must see her up close. I went to the area I stalked...I mean spotted her on camera and could not see her anywhere. I went through a few aisles and then there she was, squatting down putting some items on a shelf. I, as usual, was too obvious in my approach of setting myself out to speak to her and I could hear myself rehearsing some cheesy opening line until she just smiled and said Hi. I said Hi and told her my name and that I was new and didn't meet everyone yet and didn't recognize her from the days I have been working. She said she only worked certain days and was most likely busy and does not do register so usually out of sight. Her name was Nereida, she went by her middle name because at least back then in those days, she told me she could not stand her first name, Luz, that she now goes by years later. She looked like Vanity, who was part of Vanity 6, and starred in the movie The Last Dragon with Taimak. I kept it short and told her my position so if she needed anything, just ask for me. I went back to the office and continued my...work. (Tongue to cheek). I set myself out to spot her at least once a day and if she was near those phones on the poles, I would look up the extension of that department and call her on it. I would tell her where to look up to wave and say hi. She would look at that camera like she was looking at me, directly in my eyes and smiled like she was saying..." Bad Boy" and shook her head like she was telling me I am naughty. I am keeping this PG, so enough of that. I asked her if we could start seeing each other after work, and if I remember correctly, she had a curfew, and I would have to drive her home if she turned down a ride to join me on a date together. It went well for a while until I got her home late and her mother was waiting at the front door and ordered her in. She looked at me and said, goodnight Mr. Devine, with the PR accent, (Misster Deee-vine-a). Not a good first impression for the first meet of the mom. After a while and being closer together, she opened to me about her childhood and homelife, which I will not disclose but will say that it explained her issues with trust, and intimacy while we were together. I will respectfully refrain from getting into detail, but the subject matter happens all too often in homes, whether it be physical or mental/verbal, abuse is abuse and it is a stain that you cannot remove. Although I enjoyed spending a lot of time with her, I still went clubbing with friends, I still got into scraps with loudmouths. I mentioned my friend Dave earlier that I recently reconnected with. He is the first and only person I ever tried golfing with. I think his dad either ran or owned a country club in our county. I went there to try. Not knowing there was a dress code, I had to get the most expensive polo in the world to fit in. David had witnessed a lot of Ninja Shit I pulled in our youth that I should be in jail or in a rubber room for, but never judged and laughed it off, or just said Daaang! And left it at that. I also continued with the Auxiliary and recommended Dave to join and vouched for him. A short while later, I got chastised by the ranks because Dave decided to have a little road rage with a woman who worked for the

Sheriff's office I was told and identified himself as an officer. That's at least her version. "Two Buffs, Two Buffs that act as One" can you just hear the melody? lol...

Back to the girl. I knew I was her first everything. That's what made it more exciting when we would "go out." One time, we drove to the mountain that you must take up the highway to get to Stony Point where she lived. There was an overlook rest area. It was freezing out of course "We stayed Warm". Well, the car would not start, and we called her dad to come down the mountain to us. Not good. I think I lied and said I felt it stalling so we just made it safely off the road to this curve overlook but cannot tell if it was the battery or what. It needed some fuel splashed on the whatever...fuckit...I don't know cars. My hands were pruned and freezing by standing outside, pretending to offer to help like I knew anything, if you know what I mean. After a while of dating, I switched jobs from Bradlees and started doing security at the IBMs in NJ for a firm who had the contract. Burns or something. Another snake pit of corporate high-end women for me to gawk at. I was good for a while, especially just returning from a religious pilgrimage I went on with my family when I was close with my faith. I joined a prayer group and read the bible, even at work while in the booth on the dock or main desk if it was quiet enough. I was talking about getting engaged and marrying Nereida before the trip with my family. I thought at that point, I was sure. In my mind at least. Until I got on the plane coming back and locked eyes with a girl sitting behind me who obviously did not like sitting next to this John Candy older looking fucktard so I would make faces, give gestures while he was trying to strike up conversations with her, and finally she hinted for me to meet her in the back at the bathrooms by excusing herself loudly saying to the 'Gentleman' that she really had to go to the bathroom then looked at me with a head shake pointing the way. We didn't do the cliché thousand-mile-high club thing, but we did just have a physical, hip-holding kissing session. Held hands between seats for the end of the flight then went our own ways.

My younger brother caught me holding her hand and shook his head saying, "yeah, you are really ready for engagement", I told him "I never said I was."

I stayed good for a bit, faithful to her and resisted flirting. I started hanging more at a club that allowed underage in, based in my opinion on who you know and who you blow, I guess. The Bouncer, jokingly we called 'Tiny' but was huge. Not strong but Meatloaf huge. He got used to seeing me come in, but the first time I attempted, he looked me over and pointed at me and said, 'Go Home!", I opened my credential holding wallet that had my badge and ID I thumbed over the AUXILIARY stamp with, and he then said "GO UPSTAIRS! "...lol. Never had a problem since that night until I became one. I witnessed everything from sex to open drug use to assaults on a regular basis. It was a whole new world to me now being of age finally and having more access to such places. There were cops from the department I was an Auxiliary at, hanging out in the parking lot of the club while on duty. I thought it was to just be closer when something would happen, but all they did was flirt with drunk ass girls or wait for them to leave so they had an excuse to pull them over and flirt. This is where I learned the hard way, that some Cops, just do not want to have Auxiliary, or have anyone tell them what's going on. Because they already know and don't want to be bothered. Especially today's day, you see and hear all the charges, evidence, and criminals that just get tossed and let go, and to them, it's not even worth pursuing anymore. I had "Bothered the Police on duty outside by telling them things I saw going on in the club. Drugs, fights that were continued outside, and it was like pulling teeth to convince them to investigate it or respond in any way to a conversation, never mind getting out of their car. One night at the club, I walked in the bathroom and there was one of those young heartthrob soap opera stars snorting coke right above the sink and just looked at me and offered after he said, "What's up"? I flashed my badge, threw him against the wall and knocked out anything in his hands. He was like "WTF" and walked out looking and yelling for the manager asking who the fuck I was and complained about me slamming him around. I may have been a little educated in Law Enforcement, but I had no academy or credentials that were earned, nor any knowledge of the rights people had when it came to searches etc... Just a few college courses at this point. I did the same shit when I saw a few guys fighting outside jumping a kid and then running into the arcade in front of the club in the first lot, and chased after them and dragged them out to lecture them, but WTF was I going to do after? I had no Police car or right to charge nor the ability, so I don't know what I was thinking. Everything I was told not to do or had no right to do, I went against thinking someone would help and justify that it was the right thing to do, but that never happened. After talking with the senior members of the Auxiliary that heard from the cops that hung out at the club of my antics, they wanted to press into my head that we had no authority and no right to do the things I was doing. I stayed in the Auxiliary doing the minimum hours and events from that point on.

After some time had passed, we had talked more about getting engaged and naming a date and everything. I started working weekends too when not many people were there at the IBMs unless they had some deadline or extra things to do. One executive came in and used her badge that pops a name and area on my screen. Of course, I do not recall now what her name is but back then, it was memorized to give the greeting of the day to her by name or look her up in her section to maybe walk by if I did rounds. She was like a gorgeous porcelain doll, and had that Nympho Librarian, Bad schoolgirl cliché smart executive sexy look you see on media or music videos. I made conversation a few times with her and eventually convinced her to have dinner one night. That's what it ended up being. One night. I got sick of some zinfandel wine and puked in her apartment bathroom for like a half hour. After letting me clean up, she still let me stay over, and basically attacked me, stripping both of us and went at it like she dropped a quarter in my mouth and rode me like a mechanical horse outside a market. I guess she was deprived for a while and putting too much time in at work. Glad to be the buffer for at least a one night only relief.

I had a cool supervisor, Walter, who was a retired warden of corrections somewhere. I told him my ambitions of full time Police work and he would give advice here and there when I told him about possible areas or tests I was pursuing. He knew I was not planning on working Security forever and it was a stepping stone like most guards my age would use toward a career in Law Enforcement. I told him how I wanted the triple threat deal of being a police officer who was assigned to K9 but taught defensive tactics at the academy when needed. It would stoke all my desires. Time went by, I took some tests locally and out of state and in other countries nearby. I decided to officially be engaged to Nereida and pursue all my dreams and not have to give up any goal. We had a set date, and it was closing in. The church, the Bagpipe band of my Uncle Finbar (NYPD Emerald Society) that he was one of the original founders of, and headed as Drum Major for over 45 years, as well as all guests arranged to have off and travel, if necessary, the works. I am never again going to blame anyone but myself for what took place next. I sought out Lisa, the one I dated before Nereida. I came across her mom at their house because she left her trunk wide open late at night in the driveway while I was on patrol. I knocked and her mom answered. Lisa was entertaining a male guest and called me later to chastise me about coming to the door and bothering her. She said she had a new man and he "Does What I want" in that little squeaky voice of hers. I told her I will never be a boytoy ass kisser, or pussy whipped like that guy, but I did miss just the physical responses she had to me, and the sweet cuddling and it just came over me while driving by her house to try and get that out of her, even once more. I had moved into a small apartment I had planned on having both Nereida and myself use until we figured out where I would end up career wise. Instead, I canceled our wedding 2 weeks before it was supposed to take place and stayed there in a pit of my own sorrow and self-doubt. I had Lisa come over once, of course we fucked, and about to do something, but then my father came pulling not the driveway. He never met Lisa, all he knew is that I was not right in the head, that I just canceled a wedding all were ready for and now doing nothing but bumming around. Lisa just made it to the driveway from the doorway as my father came down. He passed her and looked at her closely and said hello. He figured that she may be the landlord or relative downstairs that rented me the apartment. That's what I hoped anyway. He was not stupid, but he didn't even mention her. He told me I had mail at the house, relatives are still coming in, even my uncle with the pipers. All for me even though all was canceled as far as the wedding. I told him all can go home or not come at all and I did not want to celebrate shit or see anyone. I went, cried my eyes out with guilt mostly over hurting Nereida and her family. Her mother got me on the phone and cried hysterically, calling me an asshole and asking how I can do this? and the work. I told her I was just not ready, and that she deserved better. I should have stuck to my guns after it blew over, but here we go, another adventure. It's all-Kung Fu. Even though I canceled the original wedding date, time went by, I got a notice that I passed the written exam and would be on the list for Orange County NY for the position of Police Officer. I still had the job doing security at the IBMs in NJ. I still had the Auxiliary. I still taught privately and bounced at a few different places now before I was even of age. Nereida was working at the clothing store where I met Lisa, the timeframes may be off, but this is a general description of what takes place. I found Nereida, and I believe I got her while she was driving. I think she yelled at me and said I ruined her life and now I am going to harass her? I said no, I miss you and want to Marry you and that I was sorry I had cold feet. I know I joked and blamed one of my brothers for dangling keys in front of me and said it was not too late to change my mind but no, I wanted to take responsibility, and do the right thing since things were falling into place. We still had a church wedding but a quiet one without as much attendance at it, since most took off for the original date. I woke up in my car outside the bar I partied at the night before and whoever was next to me asked me what I was doing that day? I said getting married in 45 minutes...WHAT???!!!

I saw I had missed a thousand calls, and Nereida called again crying asking if I didn't want to marry her and where am I? I did a record time Shit shave and wipe and got there. Tadaaa! My brothers knew what I did the night before and with. I could picture one of them taking the keys out as I say my vows and dangle them if they weren't doing it already. I was a shit husband. Then and 2 more times in my life, as well as being a shit father to my 3 sons for most of their lives. But we will get into that later. Let's hope the 4th time's a charm.

Nereida and I had the reception and honeymoon night at Bear Mountain Inn and got a great deal. Why? Because during my security time there as one of my gigs at Bear Mountain, I discovered that the wedding planners were charging people for things that were supposed to be included and complimentary. Including us when we made out reservations. So, for helping in the investigation (Not disclosing how or what method) I was offered an almost fully covered compensation wedding package. The only art that was really fucked up was the DJ company we used had a last-minute call of and sent somebody who had none of the songs or playlists we requested long before the date. This wench was playing Wham and some other British, or Teen movie credit music Bullshit. My late Brother's best friend was in attendance and was a DJ and offered to take over and had all his stuff in his truck. We wanted Irish, Latin, Club and top dance hits. It turned out great. For the time being anyway. We didn't go anywhere major for any honeymoon. We stayed at the Inn, went to another resort for entertainment for a bit, and then back to normal. Work, but also had to figure living arrangements until we determined where our lives would take us. I ran into Lisa outside of Nereida's work just as she was attempting to address Nereida to confirm if we got married. I guess she found out through other means. I faced off with Lisa with my back toward Nereida and told her to back off. Lisa looked down and saw my wedding ring and gasped like she just saw a dead body, followed immediately by clenching her eyes like she just got smacked in the face and a little "OMG" whisper came out of her. She put her forehead against mine and said, "How could you?" I simply told her I was sorry if I was not enough for her before, but I had moved on. Nereida swore I kissed her while we were talking close face to face but that was not the case. Did I want to, that's another story. We lived at her family's house for a while, and I would retain the apartment I had closer to work until we moved into it. I got along with her mother greatly, but her father was another animal altogether. We would have a few light conversations or words on subject matter, but most of anything he had to say, was just bumbling stupid man-child garbage that I would have to ignore or correct him, and her brother when they "Acted Out" That seemed to be a regular theme in my life and experience with 2 sets of in-laws. I convinced her father at one point to let me teach during good weather in the back yard that was very spacious. It was mostly people's kids, if any at all. One day, one of my coworkers from IBM Security came over to learn. He was Hispanic (Puerto Rican) like my wife and her family and struck up conversations with her mother occasionally while waiting for me for work or during workout breaks. I remember that her mother told me once that he obviously was not forced to speak Spanish in his family because his dialect was very formal classical school type of Spanish, or he just liked to embellish or elaborate more than the average person. She gave me the hint that she thought he was maybe light in the heels, to be more honest. After a few weeks of training my coworker and friend, there was one night, after he left the house, that my father-in-law was on one of his usual benders, that I am convinced to this day was more than just drinking. He had a screaming fit followed by some sounds like either he was hitting something or someone. My mother-in-law came down the stairs and into the kitchen, and I caught her with her head down crying. I tried to offer comfort and inquired as to what happened? She would not look up and waved to sort of Shue me away while a shaky whisper of "Go Away" came twice with each wave of her hand. I was furious and the superhero cop persona but darker came flushing in my veins. I marched upstairs and shook the walls with my voice telling him off and that I would arrest him myself if I could. I told him I was sick to death of the miserable atmosphere he created and kept going in that house. He just took off his glasses, rubbed his eyes like he just woke up, and calmly switched the subject, or really revealed what he was angry about. He told me "Terry, I agreed to let you teach in the backyard, but only children, no full-grown men are going to be at or in my house." I didn't understand his thinking at the time, or reasoning whether it was a cultural "Machismo" thing or just a general respect thing. But...it was his house and I just said "fine, but you come to me if you have a problem, and not take it out on your wife or daughter and I am aware of all the shit you and your son have pulled on this family and I will not let it happen" Again I will not get into details out of respect. He waddled downstairs and sat in the little dining area waiting for his servant (wife) to serve him café' and whatever food she prepared. I told her we had an understanding and she said just sit and eat and everything is fine. I told her something to the effect that "It better be for now on" and then no more than a few seconds later, my father-in-law threw some shit around and started a Spanish only cursing fit and argument. Later I found out that it was about how he thought she told me everything about him, his habits or business in that house. I told him to sit down or calm down and warned him I would throw him out if he didn't stop. He summoned his son, who was a juicer (Bodybuilder type, not shake maker). His son came flying down the stairs with a big bat looking stick of some sort, and before he could even reach the bottom step, I warned him that I would break that shit over his head after I took it from him and that he knew damn well that this had to stop. He looked at me and I could see the wheels turning in his head evaluating my words and the situation he could be facing with me. (Getting his ass kicked) He lowered the stick and said, "It's not your place to get involved". I said that someone had to be the man of the family and it obviously was not either of them.

Chapter six
"FROM 'BUFF' TO 'ROOKIE"

I decided it was time to move us both into the apartment I had before we legally got married that was closer to my work and we would still half ass live between both families in between depending on what was going on that week and where. Nereida told me a story of a Shepard she had and missed. I too, loved dogs and especially would love having a German Shepard. I went and found a breeder after checking multiple ones that had reputable bloodlines and even ranked in top show dog competitions. I picked a male puppy that was the son of a well-known Northeast Champion show dog named,' Caramia'. I named him 'T.J.' Not named after me like it was 'Terry Jr.' but after a Police character that William Shatner played named "TJ Hooker" because he was the strong one and dominant from my observation of the litter. Some time went by, and I was obsessed now with training TJ, and reading K9 books that covered everything from obstacles, to searches, to stories of successful utilization of deploying dogs in Police work, which was one of my goals. I signed up for West Virginia K9 College and enrolled and ICS Veterinary Science to have transcripts if not a degree at least and knowledge to put on a resume for when I apply for that position within any department I may join or be accepted to. It was like 1989, so there were still slides to have to look at and workbooks, not laptops and I had to learn about a lot of animals, not just K9. It was hard but it gave me a Tech level diploma and helped later in my career. TJ grew fast. My father would tell me that I cared more about that dog than I did my own wife. I thought he was kidding but deep down, I don't think he was by what he had seen in my behavior. TJ and I were joined at the hip, and I invested a lot into him. The toys, the collars, the training, and the nutrition supplements were equal with spoiling a high end and high maintenance date. Nereida and myself were fighting, between family disputes, her

'Trust issues' and some other Psychological shit she had going on, and to top It all off, the landlord was complaining about our dog TJ making howling and banging noises mixed with barking all day upstairs while we were both at work, so I started taking TJ with me to work until one weekend I was caught letting him rest inside the IBM behind my desk, and I was facing termination. Not too long after that, I was fired.

I got the call I was waiting for. A Chief of Police from Town of Wallkill in Orange County NY called me and said I was selected off the list and asked if I was interested in joining the department. I of course went for the interview, and I accepted. He told me until the next class in the academy would start, I could still be on the road with a training officer as a probationary Police officer. This could not have happened at a better time, because I had hardly been making any money, on the shit list at the Police department's Auxiliary and in the doghouse with the wife. I went ahead of her and got us set up in a community type living apartment complex in Middletown NY minutes from the Police Department. I was not satisfied with TJ's progress in training and saw that this department had no K9 unit. I had brought TJ to a trainer and wanted him to try to get him stronger because he was not growing any bigger for some reason. He would use a pinch collar, do some obstacles and have a regiment of supplements he had advised for his growth and strength. I was an impatient man and wanted to be quickly considered for a K9 slot if there would be one. I did some research of anyone selling an already trained K9 in search, Narco, and patrol. There was one in Marinette Wisconsin, a female Shepard named Zest whose owner was a Police Officer K9 Unit trainer and made an offer for me to come out and spend a week working with the dog. It was a great deal and a great price. Zest was a great tracker and would go from playful to straight up aggression on one word demand. It was amazing. I passed the course; did miles of tracking in a blizzard they had and still found all targets of people and narcotics set out. This did not give me credentials of course but it did give me a certified trained dog to use when the time comes. It was my endeavor to do that. I started patrolling later that month after being issued uniforms but noticed that we were issued revolvers with speed loaders? This is how far back this department was. Basketweave styled belts and leather, the range was in the woods outside just to pop off some shots, and that was that. I hit the road with my Field Training Officer (FTO) John, daily, and rotated with him to night shift when that happened. His regular partner, whose name escapes me, started asking me if I knew what was going on with the Department at the current time. I had no idea of course, not only being the new guy, the rookie, but also new to the area. He told me about how the Chief that hired me is on the way out, and that a new chief is coming in that is a former State Police Investigator. He told me the Feds are investigating the department and that the department was not under or not certified under some recognized and required State and Federal approving board. I noticed that most of these officers had side jobs. I thought it was for the extra money, but maybe it was for a backup in case they were told they no longer are a Cop. Here anyway. A few months passed and all that I was told would happen had happened. I started the Academy, which was back down in Rockland County, at the fire training center in my original hometown minutes from my family. It is a good thing I moved up to Middletown because they insisted on us reporting to the station and driving one of the patrol cars to the academy and having to return it daily after refueling. If I still lived down there during training, I would have to drive over 45 minutes minimum each way 3 trips a day. About 3 months into the class, I was told we could still patrol when they needed extra bodies on off days for details or patrol. There was a flex time requirement from the officers but not really us as cadets. This banked hours when we would volunteer for that extra little bit. One of the officers that was one of the originals hired, and a PBA treasurer (Police Benevolent Association) union representative too, told me a new Chief had taken over and was bringing some of his own people in and changing stuff immediately as far as personnel.

The new chief started and introduced himself to us in a meeting before we went on the trip to the academy one morning. He looked like he was trying too hard to look like Sam Elliot but looked more like the Monopoly Mayor mixed, with a big silver mustache and as much hair to hold onto. Whenever you would start any question or statement or talk at all, he would raise his head, bite his lip and squint analyzing you at the same time. Interrogation 101 habit. He also would act like he didn't hear you by turning to the side offering one ear to you while his eyes and expression looking confused at whatever it is you are talking about. Like you were crazy or speaking another language, and he was seeing if you were going to finish. Also, a technique used in interviews or interrogation to give the impression you are analyzing if the truth is coming out of the subject's mouth and to look skeptical. I only know this, because he did it to me. Here is how that went. One day, he called us all into a conference room, including all officers and cadets to announce a current situation. A girl went missing, possibly abducted. He mapped out areas that we would do a grid search walk through to start in the search. During his talk, I got anxious to offer my dog to help and turned to my FTO, John, to ask his opinion. John kept his eyes on the chief and shrugged his shoulders at my suggestion, so I repeated, "Should I ask, should I ask?", I got startled when the chief loudly addressed me and asked, "Do you mind if I finish?" Thank you very Much" in a total enraged expression and tone. I nervously chuckled and said, "Go ahead, Jesus and turned to John like I was saying "You believe this guy?". The meeting ended and I thought about my interruption and bad impression with the chief. I apologized and told him I just wanted to offer help with a search dog I had. He told me, (with the expressions I talked about before): "Terry, I said to myself that he is young (Me) and he is a rookie and doesn't know better, so I get it." He turned down my offer and told me he does not like Shepherds', and he will bring in Rottweilers, if and when he will have a K9 unit. I was crushed. But it was what it was. We did our little show for the family and town by doing the walk search and to this day, I still do not know what came of it. The few I drove to the academy from our station were 2 male officers and a female. Apparently, the female was the daughter of a State Trooper Investigator who worked with or knew the current chief, so it was fair to say, her job was safe. We all became close and participated in events at the station when they came. I remember "being volunteered" as that year's Santa Claus being the first new rookie, and having a belly, which I always did no matter my regiment. There was also a hot dispatcher that would catch my eye once in while signing out the vehicle and was very sweet but an obvious flirt. I would think to myself of how many of these guys she had been with before my arrival, so I kept it professional, never mind having a wife. On that note, let me tell you another "No Shit" moment.

The officer I mentioned earlier, that was the treasurer and PBA rep, also worked for the local phone company more than he did for the Police Department and for a longer time. I told him that the female I went to the academy with, and the dispatcher were getting hang up calls and one had done a caller ID check, and it was made from my apartment but while I was working night shift. I told them and now him, that it was not me, and I think my wife was making calls to them to see if I was really on duty or with them fooling around or something. I asked if he could put a trace on my line or get me a record of calls for that whole month. He did. I waited until the next time I heard the same story from the females, or direct accusations while arguing with my wife before I whipped out the record of calls made by her while I was on duty. I asked her in the middle of the argument that night, what did she do while I was working? She said she talked to her parents on the phone then just went to bed. I showed her the multiple calls she made to every female name on our department's roster and that I was fully aware of her antics. I told her that all she had to do was call dispatch and ask to have me come by when I had the chance, that there is a code used on the radio to make contact to our homes, as to not let everyone know your business. I told her I know she was raised not trusting males, because (without getting into detail,) she did not exactly have the best role models at home between her father or brother's abuse that she witnessed and experienced. That was it for me, I had enough and told her to move back in with her parents until we figured out what to do and where we stood. After another month, I was in such a state of depression, I turned back to going out to local clubs, drinking, dancing, and fucking around, to include my fellow female classmate. That was only a quicky, maybe twice, and a night with the dispatcher in her car. During my months on the job so far, I have had traffic incidents, warrants to serve, burglary and robbery calls, and a lot of domestic violence calls. One domestic call was during a heavy snow and ice storm. I was partnered with my FTO, John and it was upstairs in a multi-unit type apartment complex. Domestics are one of the most dangerous calls you can arrive at because you are stepping to the unknown 90% of the time. It is mixed with emotions flying sky high and you never know what's going to happen when one sees you taking away the other even if they are the ones who called for help against that person. This held true on this night. As protocol, we would walk in, separate the couple or multiple parties and make sure they are in eye of each other so they don't think there is any side taking or abuse to the other going on but most of all to assure officer safety so we can see each other, then, we compare notes in the middle while the tenants' chill. As soon as we are determined by any evidence, admission or obvious abuse, we take the guilty party or most violent out by handcuffs and do the whole process. In this case and as most cases, the husband was the one called about, by his wife and went after her as we entered the apartment. As soon as we cuffed him, she came flying after us screaming to let him go to include a few punches and kicks. My FTO grabbed her before she could make it to me escorting him out and slammed her against the wall and down to now arrest her. While walking down the stairs, an adult male came out of the apartment below and started up the stairs cursing at us claiming we were "Real tough guys" arresting a woman and other Bullshit. He, and the whole neighborhood could hear her screaming, narrating all we were doing or making up some shit to get attention. I warned the guy to back off and go back to his apartment. He still came up the stairs blocking our way and clenched his fists cursing me out and challenged me by saying "Why don't you try taking me outside mother fucker?" I will end this story with this, the guy may still have a size 10 boot print still on his chest. I started working out to continue my Tae Kwon Do training, and help teach, if need be, at a local Dojang because it was the only school and style nearby. The owner and head Instructor was the first female I have ever learned from formally. Older but fit and skillful and brought me up knocking off the dust to my next level during the year to learn more required forms for my 4th dan because I have been putting off testing for a while and too many breaks in between because of life events.

There was one place I enjoyed while off, and that was at the movie theater down from the department. Everything was on the same strip. I would flash my tin or give a business card with my badge number on the Patch logo design and get in for free. A lot of food places also comp for Police. One time, in front of a "Date", a huge security guy in a black suit came straight up to me and whispered, "No more business cards or flashing you fucking badge, you pay like everybody else". I just nodded in agreement and thanked him like it was the last time he would deal with me. My vehicle still had all the buff shit I started installing when I was an Auxiliary. Like a red bubble magnetic light, mesh removable gate type window dividers for when I have my dog in the car, like a K9 Mobile, and a PA system so I could speak without leaving my car, and of course a CB/Scanner combo to hear Police frequencies for anything I may want to help with if off duty and it arises. I still had that 24/7 cop mode in me and could never stand seeing violators of law just blatantly happen without saying or doing something. So, I was always prepared. I figured volunteer firemen have theirs, to race to and attend and help at a scene, so why should I be any different, especially since I was now "A real Cop". This point and fun fact I told you about is going to play a part in a little while, so get ready, because it's going to be the incident that plunged me into another life.

I went to another club frequently and became friendly with the bouncer there. He had a son just as big as him and it looked more like they could be brothers. I showed them a lot of "Camera friendly moves" I call them with a mixture of Aikido, Jitsu and the usual Cop come along moves I taught. Steve Seagal was popular with the Above the Law movie and these guys were eating it up. I told them they are simple but look advanced because Seagal was an expert and did those white belt moves so long, they looked advanced. I figured hey, some of these cops are working other jobs, why can't I make a few bucks teaching or bouncing on weekends when I was not attending the academy. I didn't carry my weapon, personal or issued while I was doing security at the bar or clubs. I kept it under my driver's seat in my car that I parked in the same lot as the patrons but closer to the main door to keep an eye on it. One night, a fight broke out, it was getting to be a bigger daisy chain of people getting involved, hit and hitting back by the original source causing it all by their tossing around stuff and each other. I must have elbowed my arm barred and thrown out at least 6 guys myself and the father son team was getting tackled in a ball of wrestling resisting assholes. It was a confusing interlock of multiple guys that I accidently grabbed, and wrist locked one of the other bouncers instead of the ones fighting, that's how balled up like a cartoon they were. We were able to get these last fucktards outside, but the fights continued. One smaller dude was banging his chest and challenging us, while snorting his blood-filled nose, most likely from my elbow, and spitting huge balls of bloody phlegm at our feet. After a while of telling him to go home and warning of calling the police, he smashed my passenger window of my car with his fist yelling C'MON! I was more worried about him getting my weapon than I was about the window. I told him he was under arrest, and he just laughed and drove off. I went in my car, put my red bubble light on my hood and chased him to the movie theater lot but he left there speeding back onto the highway. I knew I would be in trouble if I reported that I was working as a bouncer, I knew that I would be in trouble if it was known I fought and hit someone. I knew I would be in trouble if I was reported pulling someone over with my personal vehicle. But...I did those things, thinking that nobody involved would report it, because they would be in trouble themselves. That was not the case. I got called into the Chiefs office, and with all the interrogative expressions I described earlier, he asked me not to lie to him and inquired about a complaint given about me driving after someone, speeding, using my red light and thru a parking lot. I lied, denied it, said it must be someone that didn't like me. He dismissed me and the inquiry for a little while and let me go about my week. I was halfway through the academy by this point. Nereida came up to get a few things, visited and helped with the dogs while I was waiting on the Chief to get back with me, thinking it would blow over but warned her that it was serious and may have to have a backup plan if we were to stay together. Sure, fucking enough, upon arriving back at the station after class and signing the vehicle log, the dispatcher told me the Chief wanted to see me and not to go home yet. The meeting took 5 minutes without one word allowed to be spoken or heard from me. Chief came into the office and said "Terry, I asked you the story and told you not to lie to me, well, you lied to me. The Civil Service says I don't have to have any reason or tell you why, but we do know a few good reasons, but you are hereby terminated." I asked if I could finish the academy to at least get certified and maybe get to another department by having the diploma. Chief said "No, you no longer represent the Town of Wallkill Police so you cannot attend anymore." (It would be 15 months later that I found out, that was not the truth or the case at all.) I took off everything I had and handed it in. The chief asked me if I had my duty weapon, since I was still in uniform. I told him it was at my apartment and the staff at the academy told us not to be armed while attending. He told me he would meet me at my apartment to get it. I told him I would go ahead of him since my wife was there and make sure all was smooth. The chief knocked on my door, and my female K9 Police Dog Zest started barking and stood stiff watching him. I gave the word "Friend" and she laid down and panted friendly with her tongue out and allowed him in the doorway. I told him that is the dog that is fully trained as you see. He looked at me a little nervous, like he wondered if I would give the attack command. Chief asked me if I had personal weapons. I said yes but I I had a permit for all the county and surrounding and he will not take any weapon besides what was issued and don't flatter himself, I am not going to kill myself over his little corrupt, uncertified department.

From that point on, I could not afford the rent, the bills, or any last payments I had a contracted agreement to make on Zest, my K9. It stated that any missed payments would be a forfeiture of ownership and she would have to be returned at my expense. I did not have the money and had to borrow from my 3rd oldest brother Dan to send her by flight in a Vari Kennel back to the original officer and owner I got her from. No other deal was agreed to, and he lost patience because I was late a few times with payments. She was worth over $12K. I had at least 3 more payments to make that I could not, and I had to borrow over $2K to send her back. One of the most expensive mistakes I had made in my life. At that point anyway. I had started moving back down to Rockland County to stay with my parents since me and Nereida were still not cool with each other nor was I with her family. I donated TJ to a breeder/trainer who I believe donated him after full training to a Police Department somewhere or to a Cop. My parents would not welcome the dogs and did not have that kind of set up or desire to have them there. I thought I lost everything, and all was lost and remember nodding to myself that this was all because of my ego and bad decisions. I was just not satisfied with the opportunity given and took it for granted and advantage in other aspects. I knew I had to grow up and get back to what else I did know about. Fighting. I emptied the apartment of the last bit of stuff and traveled to the local mall. There I saw what the answer would be. The very thing that represented all I believed in and taught about. Defend yourself and others for your community and spread those teachings and skills for defending the whole country. I met a recruiter for the United States Army!

Chapter Seven

"EXIT THE WANNABE- ENTER THE WARRIOR"

I met a United States Army recruiter, a Staff Sergeant (SSG) who was handing out cards and other brochure type material with all the information and cool action pictures of repelling, jumping, marching, the works. I told him I was aware of what was going on overseas at the time and I wanted to be a part of the 'Gulf war', that I was a fighter, an instructor, and until recently, a half ass cop that needed something real fast. He invited me to come to his office the next day where he showed me what I would have to do after taking the ASVAB (Armed Services Vocational Aptitude Battery) test to see what jobs or level I qualified in. I wanted to be RAMBO! all the Special Force, Weapon experts kill everyone bad dude with every specialty skill like Air, Sea and land invasion tactics and go fight. You know, the usual answer one would give during those times and as a patriot. The recruiter asked me why I wasn't a cop anymore or trying with that. I told him I needed to grow up and everything I was told by my father, and seniors on the jobs I have had, including the Auxiliary and about what impression I made , or what to do or not do, ended up being right and I lost my job from being what they said I was in interviews with former employers when I went for jobs that require a background and reference check. I was overzealous. The SSG did a height and weight check on me, and said by Army standards, I was obese. I said "Well, no shit, you haven't changed your standards since Vietnam and want a guy my height to be below 185lb and starving looking like they all looked like in any footage you see." I was a 228lb fat ass typical donut eating cop but still kicked ass at Martial Arts and fast. He put me on the delayed entry program which was the time it would take to meet all standards and requirements before being able to be shipped off somewhere. I asked Nereida for help studying because there was more advanced math and such on the ASVAB test than I learned in school. She was smart at that and always got great grades. Within 2 weeks I got the hang of the algebra that I saw examples of on the practice test book I used to prepare for the ASVAB. I scored high enough for Engineer/construction and Military Police as two main MOS (Military Occupation Specialty). The SSG said I could always try for other jobs and specialties later in my service but to jump in on the Military Police (MP) one since that was my experience and interest in the civilian world anyway. He cheesed it up and said "Yeah, you are like a cop in every part of the world for the US Army with worldwide authority, and in every state. I was sold and signed the first set of documents and the final ones when I met all requirements and my wait to go to MEPS (Military Entrance Processing Station) was over. Signed the final dotted line and swore in and left on Veterans Day, which seemed fitting. I was now property of the United States Government and they let you know that right away. Boot camp was at Ft. McClellan Alabama. I was part of Bravo Company 795th 2nd Platoon. I was used to the kind of hurry up and wait atmosphere from the little bit of the Police Academy I did attend, and with instructors who acted like Drill Instructors. You would figure being a cop, an instructor, having some experience, and used to being surrounded by a group of yelling pushy idiots (My Brothers...lol), that I would not be fazed at all with whatever they, the Drill Sergeants, had to dish out ..right?..WRONG! I was smoked (Put through multiple rigorous disciplinary exercises) every time I even blinked. Dropped for push ups one second, Monster Stomping the next, burpees and squats forever and then back down for push ups for even one hint of talking, even if it's to answer their own questions. I got it eventually and learned that in order to make you all equal, and as one unit, with nobody standing out as different, you must be broken down to be built back up equally and together the same way to assure continuity, consistency, and have that bond of teamwork. That was always a challenge to achieve right away and took a long time with us, a bay of

53 men I was to share all training, latrine, chow and any disciplinary actions or drama with. One of the first days of arrival, I was standing in formation, and we were all to start memorizing our General Orders from our (What they called) 'Smart Books', which was a manual of basic tasks for a soldier during basic training. Everything from drills to field missions and weapons, nomenclature etc. We were to recite our General Orders on command at any given time. Like "I will guard everything within the limits of my post and not quit my post until properly relieved" and such. We had a female Drill Instructor in charge of the female platoon, but all were allowed to drill you any time they deemed fit, and you answered in the same manner of "Yes Drill Sergeant!" This Drill Instructor was gorgeous. Looked Asian mixed with either Latin or American Indian. Found out she was married to the senior Drill Instructor of Delta Company so there was no way of even hinting interest without getting killed. I guess my hat was kind of off because she put her cheek next to me, turned toward my ear with her voluptuous mouth and then said in a whisper, "If you do not straighten that cover on your head, I am going to rip your head off and drop you!" I smiled and gave out an "aww, that tickled" as my response. That did it. I was surrounded by 4 Drill instructors like a kicked hornets' nest of Brim smacking Sergeants pounding my head with their drill hats every time they yelled some contradicting command one from the other. "Get up, Get Down, Jumps, Pushups, run in place, Side Straddle Hop" (Jumping jacks). One would bark another task during, after, and all in between each other. Then the usual strait from a movie line came out of our head Drill Instructor, who looked a little like Eminem the white rapper a little. He asked me, "Where are you from boy?" I went along with it and answered, "New York, Drill Sergeant". He said "Oh so you a Gangsta?", I answered "Negative Drill Sergeant, I go after Gangstas"..then all four of them stopped and you would expect to hear a skipped record scratch like errrp! Like in a movie. The head Drill Instructor faced off with me and said" What the fuck is that supposed to mean, you some dumb fat kinda Bounty

Hunter or somethin? I answered," I was a cop Drill Sergeant". That just made all of them go nuts and yell out excitingly, like "Oh Boy, watch out, what we got here? it's the Law" They poked at my stomach making fat jokes and said shit like "Should have known that doughnut eating tummy," and such. The head Drill told me to get into the CQ (Command Quarters) office and wait there. I waited until they were done dismissing the rest of the platoons to return to their bays until further notice. The head drill came flying in with another Drill. He smiled and said, "You really a cop". I told him I used to be and that a new chief came in and fired a lot, I was on probation and had no say, and it was a small department and so forth. He stopped me and asked if I had training. I said yes of course. He said, "Then you know the game and how it's played and now, you are responsible". The Drill Instructors chuckled and said "You are now the Platoon leader" while doing some mouth sound effects like a royal knighting was taking place with horn playing sounds and put a Sergeant striped band on my arm and Velcroed it closed. "When they fuck up... Devaine, Daveen, Devine, whatever yo fuckin name is, it's all on you. In fact, I am going to call you 'Dan'..Dan Devine like the Notre Dame coach..how do you like that..Dan?".. I said "Real Original Drill Sergeant" (NOT).."I like It fine"(NOT)!

"Fuck my life" I said to myself. Now of course as I walk into the bay, all of them surround my bunk and ask the expected questions. "What happened, you were a cop? What's that on your arm? How old are you? Why are you here? I told them all a brief version of who I was and where I came from and why. From that point on, I was known as the grandpa of the group being the oldest and I guess experienced. Also now, they all called me 'Dan' because of the Damn Drill Sergeant. These guys hardly held a woman, never mind a weapon, so it was up to me to assure, at least for a little while, that they stayed on track or it's all our asses, but really mine I was worried about more. Our Drill Instructor's mere presence commanded respect. He was sharp, competitive and a little deviant when he wanted to be. He would be that kind of mentor that is the hardest and most disciplinary, but you end up respecting and listening to them the most because there was no questioning or reproach to his style of leadership, and it produced results. We outshot the other platoons on the range, we as a platoon, won a drill competition D&C (Drill and Ceremony) that consisted of marches. Traditional and custom-made ones with clever cheers like, "Second Platoon, we are the best, if you try to beat us, we will put you to rest, D&C, M16 (Rifle), Law Dogs! (Our Company sign) Killers in Green!". About halfway into our training months, the Head Drill Instructor went to compete against other Drill Instructors for the Drill Instructor of the Year award. It was global, not just statewide. He came back and was cursing that he took second. He would nod and pout and just hiss like "ccccc, second sucks" then say a few remarks about the guy who came in first and won it, like it was stolen from him. I Don't doubt it.

When you work alongside people, you start to get comfortable, especially when you all are sharing the same experiences no matter how differently one responds to it than the other. You learn each other's outside talents or a glimpse at their normal life of what they left or have at home, but who was left too. You find out who the bullshit artists are, the pranksters, the playboys, and talented ones like musicians or who could carry a tune. Two privates ran a little fuck-fest rotation with the willing recruits from the female platoon. They would meet in the middle of the night in the laundry room and go at it. I walked in on one "Session" they were having and was disappointed to find one female was one I really thought was innocent and sweet, but I should have known better. Horn dogs. This became even more frequent when we had inserts come through. Inserts were regular Army Noncommissioned Officers like Corporals, Sergeants ranked from E5 or E6 (Enlisted levels) that decided to switch jobs and become MP qualified. The females went star struck and set themselves out to hang with the experienced soldiers like it was going to get them somewhere. It just got them fucked in every

DEVINE 'KUNG FU' INTERVENTION

way and in trouble. There are also the recruits that are hygiene nightmares. Slobs, lazy, dirty, smelly pieces of crap who do not care who says anything about their filth and stay in their own funk. One soldier we finally had enough of, was one who would wait until we already cleaned and polished the latrine (Bathroom), step last minute out of his bunk, go into the latrine and fuck it all up by pissing in the toilet, leaving piss drips all over and not clean it, and then just wash his dick in the sink, leaving hairs and all funk but never take a shower. The rest of us, who couldn't take any more and to avoid us failing inspection ever again, finally decided to toss this slug into the shower and hose him down to teach him a lesson. The other wiseass slob, who also liked to talk shit, we called Tallywacker. I paid back by putting shaving cream in his boots to hear him scream out in the pitch dark and quiet when stepping out of bed to do fire watch one night. Out of 52 other recruits, he knew to yell my name somehow, lol. I guess he thought about my warning. Another hero cost us a weekend pass on base by trying to hide Snicker bars and other candy in his locker, so as the acting Platoon leader, it fell on me to "Correct this". So, I had a heart-to-heart talk with that soldier and sat with him on his bunk, telling him I understand what he is going through. I had opened a foil full of "Chocolate" (Really...Ex-lax), and told him he could finish it since we were in trouble anyway and may as well get rid of it. I knew we had a 15-mile road march coming that day since our pass was taken and the Drill Instructor was pissed. He warned me it was coming and made sure all were ready when it came time. It was payback time, and this fat fuck Choco fiend was going to learn his lesson. Every 15 minutes on that march, Mr. Snicker bar had to dive into the woods, or bush to shit his brains out. We kept him hydrated and hinted that it was never going to happen again if he was truly sorry. Lastly you also have undercover Ninjas like I found in one soldier. His name was Matt, just like my now deceased Father and brother. He was a quiet guy that I would sometimes catch just sitting on his bunk in his PT (Physical Training) gear on, but with his Kevlar Helmet on his head (Bucket) like a commercial you see of a kid imitating his dad by putting on his big shoes or hat. I set myself out to hang with him because I knew there was something about his aura that was familiar. I was right, after chatting with him and talking about what we do at home, I found out he was a Martial Artist. We would play around with Judo lifts halfway for pictures, do forms outside in the open parade area while policing the grounds, and clean our weapons while talking shop. One time, right before our last PT test, we sparred lightly, mostly fooling around. I did a spinning back kick and caught him in his ribs that were wide open unintentionally. He went down in a fetal position right away and was in obvious pain. I was hoping it was just the wind knocked out of him. He toughed it out for a while. The day came for the last PT test and after a lot of painful sit-ups, he passed the last PT test. I have connected with him recently also on social media and learned he had a broken rib that did not heal right from that incident. Sorry forever dude.

AIT (Advanced Individual Training) was next. Where we are now going to be in less of a Boot Camp setting, getting smoked and yelled at, but now more of a classroom environment but still was expected to march, and conduct ourselves as disciplined soldiers following all guidelines, we had embedded into us now. But first, before we started AIT, we had a 2 week break to go to our home of record for Exodus leave during the holidays. I think it was Christmas. I went from 228lb to 173lb within 9 weeks before leave. It helped me overall with things like my speed, which I was timed at 12:23 for the two-mile run, and I could spin and kick faster, as we had found out the hard way. I went home to Rockland NY to my parent's house and met up with Nereida who I went back and forth with written letters agreeing to try to work it out. For the time being, it was ok. It was weird being back, drinking and eating some normal tasting food that had flavor and not being monitored. I had all the cheesy novelty MP shit as far as sweaters, Army logo shit, Jacket with patriotic sayings etc. I decided to go to the mall and hang out to see a movie, eat at the food court, anything to get a sense of normalcy again before having to head back down south. I came to the escalators, and then I spotted the Sergeant from the Police Department who demonstrated and got me interested in Police Defensive Tactics instruction. He didn't recognize me right away because I was still sporting the shaved head from basic training. He asked me: "What the hell happened to you at the academy, why did you leave?".

(Remember I told you earlier, that I found out when the chief told me I no longer could attend the academy? Well, here are the facts on that.)

I told the sergeant the whole story with the chief at Wallkill, and what I had faced and told what I could and could not do, and that I joined the Army out of desperation of having a job, and income if I could be good at it.

The sergeant said "Terry, you didn't have to leave the academy. The state paid for that slot, not your chief. It was already paid for, and especially him being the new chief, he has nothing to do with it. You could have worn the Rockland County Police sweats, or cargos and finish the academy and gone with another department since you would have been certified." I was blown away and in shock. He asked me how long I had in my commitment to the Army. Told him at least five years. He looked at me and chuckled and said, "well, guess I will see you in 5", gave me a two finger to hat salute and waved goodbye. Oh well, "It's All-Kung Fu". There are forces we can control and ones that we cannot.

So, I was recharged and ready to go back. I had my share of family time, some rekindling with the wife, and some good food and drink. Got back to the base, and immediately after all of us were accounted for, it was a surprise weigh in. I could tell this was a regular rehearsed, let's feel like shit moment the Drills love to pull on recruits returning from leave. I weighed in at 193lb. The Drill Instructor was like "Daaamm Devine, we were making progress, what happened?". I said, "Normal food not measured and drinks with flavor". I lost that weight quickly because we marched to AIT every day, still had PT runs of a minimum of 5 miles each way, and back to fat boy program premeasured (One scoop of slop instead of two) small meal portions at the chow hall and forced hydration. We were now treated a little more like humans now, not barked at or as closely monitored with the Drills down our necks. We got broken down and built back up as one. We went through all drills, drama, team building and field exercises together and coped with each other's personalities and learned to work together as one unit. WE were given freedoms when earned by doing what was expected of maintaining our lockers, floor, uniform, and our task book memorized to recite at any request to do so and execute. During PT runs, we were now allowed to be called out to lead in cadence songs to motivate the platoons by repeated verses of empowering description of who we are, where we come from, and even singing stories of MOS (Military Occupational Specialty) that we had nothing to do with like Airborne Rangers, and Combat Infantry, demolitions, but it was still motivating and fun and kept your mind off the pain in your legs and losing breath. It actually develops your endurance and breathing if you can sing at the same time without a hiccup while running, then you have reached a level of conditioning far better than most that just give up any activity after school sports is done, than any gym going treadmill hamster doing the daily, and you had a whole team now you grew with to pick you up or take the lead when you have exhausted all you had. I have to say though the biggest disappointment and surprise to me, was the lack of hand-to-hand combat we did during the "Boot" phase of our training. It was the typical Police academy rehearsed compliant armbar, come along, wristlock crap you have two days to apply type of Bullshit. We had the pugil pit (Simulation of rifle bayonet training) with thrusts, slices and stabs and very little hand to hand combat. I would actually supplement what was lacking by showing some techniques up in the bay, but of course the others were reluctant in going outside the limited box of "The Manual". You will see, later, that this has not changed much even after a decade. I don't know if it's because of liability or just time management of it, but it could have been better and more.

A favorite privilege many of us liked to do if we earned a weekend or even a day pass, was to go down to the PX (Post Exchange) and buy phone cards and call home if we didn't call collect. I would always get phone cards to pay bills for my family, but it was the same cost because money in my account was put in by them anyway. I would buy the phone cards at the same time I picked up everything that had the cheesy MP logo. Stationary, mugs, T-shirts and a plaque with the Cross Pistols, or MP Corp crest with our Motto or some other inspiring words like, "Of the troops and for the troops", or "Lead the Way". I also liked to see any movie available that gave me a sense of normalcy or caught up on what I was missing in the civilian world although we were away for only 6 months. I would call home to my parents and then of course to Nereida. This was our last pass before graduation and of course, something had to spoil it for me for the rest of the day. Her mother picked up, and I could hear mumbling in the background like a short barking of attitude and could tell her mother was trying to stifle the words by pressing the receiver against her body or cupping it with her hand. When she finally agreed to come to the phone, while I waited in confusion of why she didn't want to, Nereida asked me who the hell have I been fucking? and said it must have been some whore because I gave her Crabs while I was home on Exodus leave.! I couldn't believe what I was hearing, and of course I denied it because it was the truth. I did not participate in any of that laundry room love crap, nor did I seek out any local whore while on pass, which now that I recall we had none before leave, so even more reason not to doubt me. I told her I would go get checked out while I still had time off. She still didn't believe me, but we ended the call semi cordial. I immediately went back to the CQ office to request to see the on duty medical examiner as soon as possible. The senior Drill Sergeant, a huge man with a pronounced chin like Dudley Do-Right and a voice like a Sam Elliot version of the Full Metal

Jacket Drill Instructor, came in and gave that tilted head folded arm WTF do you want warning look with his eyes piercing through me. I told him what I had learned from my wife, and I could tell he was holding in laughing his ass off, and just removed him Brim hat and wiped his face with his bare hand like he felt a web or something, but I could tell it was t try to compose himself from bursting out in laughter. He told me I would have to change into my PT gear, and he would take me. I was just putting my sneakers on as he came into the bay and yelled my name saying, "move it Devine" and "let's go" but still pacing fast toward my locker at the same time to get me. Another freedom or privilege we were given was to finally have something personal like a photo put in our lockers. I had one picture of my wife, and one of my Shepard. Senior Drill stopped yelling and looked in my locker and just whistled a cat 'call type,' like in a cartoon of something being thrown up, and then coming down in the air. He said, "Hey Devine, I tell you what, I bet this picture came with your wallet, didn't it? This can't be your wife". I told him "It is her school picture so it was professionally done, so I know it looks that way .."Oh Shit..."Drill Sergeant"! forgetting who I was responding to and getting too laxed, I jumped up in Parade rest. (Modified attention stance with hands flushed locked behind the back and legs shoulder with apart). He told me to be at ease and lock up and we would go.

I was quickly seen by the examiner who did a black light type of test and lifted my balls and pinched and stretched the skin too to look at every part of the "Bat Wing" he just made from my sack. He told me he saw some 'Eggs Forming' and black headed types of growths, like little pimples. He said two things were present. "Yes, you do have some shit jumping around and making a circus in your pubic area, so we will give you a bottle of "RID" with a small comb unless you just shave it all and clean with it" and you also have extra testosterone pockets that form little bumps common for any excess the body produces." The doctor said, "Crabs are the most common thing that happen while here, using a bunk that has been used by thousands before you, no matter how clean the bedding is, you are sharing it and the latrine and other areas that you could easily contract them." I still had a little time on pass, so I immediately called back home to Nereida and told her what the doctor said. She said she didn't know they could bounce around like that and that I better get it taken care of and she was still upset because it really bothered her physically and mentally. The part about the extra testosterone she said was "TMI "(Too much Information).

Graduation was nearing, and we had to do a last hands-on practical test of most if not all things we learned and learned about to prove we were technically and tactically proficient in each. The majority of field type knowledge like nomenclature and use of all crew served and handheld weapons were done in stations that would rate you with a "Go" or a "No Go" which would determine if you needed a fast refresher and retest. The rest consisted of knowledge of regulations, Military Police duties and practical tactics in different scenarios with a partner as a mock patrol with different scenes to arrive at, called out on the radio by an assigned instructor. There would also be paperwork to fill out or reports made when the scenario was over to utilize the UCMJ (Uniformed Code of Military Justice) or proper Military Police regulations/codes to fill in where it would ask what charges are being made, in accordance with etc... After passing all hands on and academic requirements, it was time to get ready for graduation day. We had rehearsal of marching, selected cadences, told the order of speakers and any awards given or special recognitions. After we pretty much had it down, we were told we had only a few hours to make any arrangements for families by booking a hotel downtown near the base, and to be back at a certain time that evening. Not really an open pass, but it was to get shit done. My credits from Veterinary school and the few credits transcript from college came in I sent for, giving me enough points to be promoted to an E2 for now, which is represented with one chevron, mosquito looking stripe on my uniform sleeves, and then E3 Private first class (Hollow Raindrop looking patch) when I get to my first duty station. They couldn't promote two ranks up at once during a training phase. Finding this out, I had to quickly take the patches to a tailor down in the PX area and put my dress uniform in for graduation to have them added ASAP. The tailor knows all dates of graduating companies and assured me it would be done within the time I needed. I had a few hours left, and my parents already booked a hotel for themselves and Nereida to share a room with me although I was not allowed to stay overnight in it. That saved some time from having to book it myself, so I went to the bowling alley to see who was around and get something to eat.

I was sitting with two other privates discussing who in their family were coming and where they thought we would be going and stuff like that. I couldn't help but notice, this one female, not from our company but obviously a recruit also on pass staring at me with a smile, crossing her legs but the top one swinging like she was pumping it up like she was anxious to get up. The two I was with got up and went to reserve a lane or something to play at least one game. This female immediately made her way over once they left and sat across from me at my table and relaxed back and crossed her legs, like I invited her for a chat to start. She resembled Stockard Channing in the face at least, when she played 'Rizzo' in the Movie Grease. She asked me if I had family coming down and if I made my hotel arrangements. I said that I did, and they were going to arrive that night. She then looked down, and traced the table with her fingers making circles, putting on a shy act and said, "So that gives us a room to use right now, for at least a little while?" To be nice, I told her that "although I am flattered and tempted, I cannot risk it and said, sorry." She then raised her eyebrows and shrugged and said, "Oh well, that's a shame," (with a grin like I was losing out) and then said, "I haven't been turned down yet" That visual put the nail in the coffin on the answer of a definite 'NO' from me. What man wants to hear and feel like the umpteenth number of cocks inside a woman and to hear her brag about it was the biggest turn off. I already had issues and I could imagine some glow in the dark shit coming out of this wench and onto me. I went to a porta john (Outhouse portable bathroom type), worked one out fast, took a dump, went and got my uniform and reported back to my company.

My family arrived, including my wife, and I could only see and talk to them briefly when they came straight to the base before going down to their hotel for graduation the next morning. The next day we were told we would see our loved ones watching in the bleachers or standing in the open parade deck areas. I had to report and get in formation to put on the show of marching in place, cadence calling, do some drills by command, then listen to the long boring speeches that you knew were repeated for every class but told like we were the first and best. I had graduated, and upon the final "Dismissed" for now, I went to my family who were taking turns between my mother and wife hugging and I forget if her mother came too but, she would have been included. My father shook my hand and patted the shoulder in that half ass hug we guys do. They had balloons and the usual poster board with my picture or some congrats theme on it. We were told we had to be back at a certain time and see our Drill Instructors who had their own after party we would attend but first, we would find out our destiny's (Duty Stations) that although we were allowed to put requests in for preferred ones, that was just wishful thinking. After my family lunch, I went and gave my Nereida a tour of the base, downtown PX area, and told her stories of who is who in my platoon and all the antics I did not cover all in written letters or phone calls. Like a Cheesedick, I also serenaded her with cadences learned, but like I usually do, as well as most of my brothers, I would use cartoon character voices and give an 'R' rated version of anything I said or sang. We were good at that. I let her know and then eventually my family, that I had to get back, and that I would not be coming home but to be directly shipped or flown really, to my first duty station that was unknown to me at the time. I don't say goodbye, I just say "See you later". I returned with the others, and we were told to hang in our bay until called to formation by our Drill Instructor. We were told to sit in place or take a knee as this would be a lengthy discussion of who, what, where, when, and why we were going to certain places and what led up to it by current events. We got the brief and assignments and now it was time to pack and get ready for the party that is going to include all us soldiers and Drill Instructors in relax mode and civilian attire because now we were 'Soldiers,' not little puke recruits or civilians. The gathering would be filled with awards and recognition to our Drill Instructors and Senior Drill that we all chipped in for and ordered in time. The usual plaques or some memorabilia to remember our time and appreciation for molding us into soldiers and MPs. The greatest privilege at the party was the request and permission by the Senior Drill to go ahead and imitate any if not all our Drill Sergeants. I didn't go first but was prepared because, behind their backs and to entertain my guys during the whole Basic Training phase, I was doing it anyway. A few privates were surprisingly good. More at the character and words used, than the voice of some Drill Instructors, but you could still tell who they were impersonating. Now it was my turn, and the whole company knew and had heard me before impersonating some, and the laughter had already begun and the usual ooo-ooohhhh shit here we go came from many too. I started of course with the one I most respected, and feared that was our Head Drill, who was second place winner of Drill Sergeant of the Year. He had a distinct "I tell you What" facial expression and piercing voice that he would repeat some words in mid-sentence like Foghorn Leghorn. I.e... I tell you...I say I tell you whuut private..and "it ain't gonna happen ain't gonna happen !". I was on a roll and already on my 4th and last after finishing my impersonations of Head Drill, Senior Drill, to include one other Drill, another asshole who threw me against a coke machine when I didn't hold my hat right reporting for pay and now it was time for this one Bulldog looking but also sized, little Drill Instructor who made up his height with attitude and being squared away. He had a raspy voice too, so it was easy. To give a hint right away of who I was imitating, I went down to my knees, and started with a question that he would start any conversation with. He would approach us during any task we were in the middle of, whether it be cleaning weapons, our bay, or just returning on foot from somewhere. He would say, "I don't know about you privates, but I would" ….and such. That was it, the whole party, Drills, guests and all including invited officers were pissing their pants on the floor busting ribs laughing. It would be our last good time for a while. Now, we were different people, a part of a time honored Corp, and it was time to take all we grew together in and learned, and execute!

"No single event can awaken within us a stranger totally unknown to us. To live is to be slowly reborn."(Antoine De SAINT-EXUPÉRY)

I will summarize and fast forward to my first duty station, post Desert Storm, after a brief description timeline of what took place and what missions MPs are tasked with during the operation. In today's society, and government, I see what heroes, all veterans, who served are facing. Criticism, disrespect, and some have gone as far as being put on trial for actions taken, or engaged in, that were assigned and ordered. Never mind the high suicide rate of veterans that go ignored and forgotten. Therefore, I will not give intimate knowledge, (details, stories, or events) that have occurred and that can be exploited and or questioned, resulting in any veteran being put in harm's way legally, or personally. I will however recognize and thank my second oldest brother I mentioned earlier, Patrick for his lifelong career service in the US Air Force and as a War Veteran. Most of the major events that started and ended Desert Shield/Desert Storm have taken place before our graduating class had been deployed to any duty station. August 1990 thru April 1991 the main events that took place were:

Saddam Hussein had invaded Kuwait. UN issues Resolution 678 calling for Iraq to withdraw from Kuwait with a deadline of January 15, 1991. The US Congress passed a resolution to use the Military Force when the deadline passed. January 17, 1991, US and coalition forces launch a campaign of air and missile strikes on targets in Iraq and Kuwait destroying Iraq's air defenses, communications, infrastructure (Military) Oil and Transportation Infrastructure. Iraq retaliates by firing missiles at Israel and Saudi Arabia. US and allied launch ground offensive/attack, Special Forces infiltrate into Kuwait and Iraq. A Scud missile fired by Iraq killed 28 Americans and 100 wounded in barracks in Khobar. Saddam announces plans to withdraw but still claims Kuwait and does not renounce. US and allied forces bomb a convoy of retreating Iraqi troops and enter Kuwait. US President Bush suspends offensive combat operation against Iraq February 27, 1991. February 28th -March 3rd, Iraq accepts UN resolutions and General Schwarzkopf's cease fire agreement. Over 22,000 Iraqis were killed, and 148 Americans killed in combat.

Military Police like myself are called 'MP' not only as an acronym, but it also stands for what some joke as "Multi-Purpose". I can tell you that this is no joke and has held true in my military career to prove so. Military Police although provide support behind friendly lines, during any combat missions they are often called upon for combat support to address:

High violence in cities or communities by enforcing dismounted patrols and providing policing in areas of high-rate violence against their people or providing a policing plan by working together or mentoring a local authority.

Processing of and watching over POWs (Prisoners of War) and refugees, after escorting Infantry, medical teams, Civil affairs, to take them in. Conduct recon of areas or routes to evaluate and determine danger levels, alternate routes, note all bridges and roads and make a protection plan in case of ambushes. Whether it be an attack or a natural disaster, MPs assist in pushing people out of their homes and get them to a new temporary location. Convoy or VIP escort and protection, Detention ops, Anti-terrorism and physical security/force protection. I had the honor to wear the patch of the 89th and 18th Military Police Brigades more than once in my Military career and reunite with some when I was deployed to Iraq later in this journey.

Fast forward: Germany. The most common place that 90 % of MPs ended up after the 'Operation' was Germany. No matter what Brigade or Regiment, there was plenty to do all over, and Germany seemed to be the go between central headquarters (Metaphorically speaking) to assure readiness to deploy. Many of us were assigned to Brigades or subordinate battalions and companies spread throughout Germany. Providing Law Enforcement, Force protection, Custom missions and many more tasks that supported USAREUR (United States Europe and EUCOM (US European Command). My first duty station in Germany was in Mainz. More than half my graduating class, well at least just the males in my class, were assigned with me to the Wackernheim Military Police Company. (WMPC). When we finally got there, we were like The Walking Dead, zombies that were exhausted and just wanted to be given our assigned barracks room and crash. Our new First Sergeant, or I should say acting First Sergeant, since he had no diamond kept him as an E7 in his rank until promoted to E8, came outside with a little hunched Bob Dillon rat boy faced looking Sergeant E5. They tried doing the continued false motivated hooah! newbie attention to orders crap but we were not having it. They asked us if we were excited to be there, to get started, for a new mission, after about a dozen pandering fed HOOAHs! from us, and after every stupid thing that came out of his mouth, the First Sergeant turned to Sergeant Rat Boy and said the obvious. He was like "Sergeant, they look tired, don't you think? Maybe it's time you give them their assigned room numbers and maybe take them to chow after they rest". Then back to us..." How does that sound privates?". Then we gave the last HOOAH! To answer as in..Fuck yeah!. And about time. He then made some faint horn sounding noise from his mouth as he looked to the side like he was passing gas..like "OOP TIN HUN "..but like a cartoon clown nose or horn on an old fashioned car. I guess some in formation understood him, because they snapped to attention, so I followed their lead and realized it was his way of saying "Group... Atten-tion!. 'Group,' is the preparatory command, and 'Atten-tion!' Is the command of execution with a separation between the first and second part of the command. Ok..enough of the lesson, bottom line, he was a cheesedick Mr. Rogers soft spoken pandering poser who hasn't had to give an order in a while and out of practice. We got to our rooms and were excused from any activity until the next morning, so most of us just went to explore what little we had on our grounds. There was a little cantina you could eat at if you didn't want what was at the chow hall, and it had a game room attached including real gambling machines that actually paid out winnings. I had a fast meal, made a point to call home and talk to family and let them know where I was and that I was ok. Although we were fine at graduation, there was still a hesitation between me and Nereida and it seemed our relationship was just a routine checking of the box with unmeaningful inquiries about each other's days or feelings and our love was just fading away between the time I left on that bus after swearing in, all the way to my new post now at this point in my life. But..those circumstances would change and be put to the test faster than planned ...stand by!

The next morning, we were given a knock on our doors to get up and dressed and report downstairs for formation within the hour after being woken. I couldn't tell if we were supposed to get chow on our own, or they were going to dismiss us to do so before any tasks were given. Our assignment and mission were to provide customs operations working alongside and monitoring German civilians with the Quality control, sanitizing, logging and inventory of all Military Equipment and vehicles returning from Operations in Kuwait and Saudi Arabia during Desert

Shield/Storm. This was a huge operation that handled everything from as small as computer chip boards, to M1 Abram tanks and all in between. But first..we had to go through a required 'Death by PowerPoint' and hands on training in Customs to officially be able to stamp, seal, sign, and tag anything and everything that was ready to be shipped out or however transported that passed all the myriad involved. This was about 168 hours of classroom and many days of hands-on inspection Do's and Don'ts, of what to look for, how to categorize, what to do with any found items left inside others i.e. (Weapons inside a tank left from war). Eventually, we were told that we would be tested and get an updated Driver's license at the motor pool to start taking ourselves to classes, and our assigned areas including the range. So, everything from a simple Pickup truck to a Deuce ½, to a Bus from 18 to 80 passenger size we trained on, and I eventually passed after hitting many flower pots off window sills of the villager living on those cobblestone roads in the towns we would practice going through. We would rotate with other companies who had L&O (Law and Order) assignments as MPs to patrol family housing areas, and ride along with the German Polizei (Police) sometimes around surrounding areas as a joint effort to assure order since we Americans were occupying and frequent business such as clubs, malls, bars, etc…we also were doing force protection and QRF (Quick reaction Force) duty down the block from our base in a little building on fenced off grounds, protecting some "Important Item". All experiences and duties were fine, but it was getting that Groundhog Day feeling of the same routine day in and day out. There was nothing to do in Mainz, at least not our little area and the cantina was only open until a little while after dinner. I got sick of hanging in the barracks even though we had a day room to play games or watch TV/Movies on DVD. We that had off at night on the weekends, finally went exploring and asked around where we could go. The most popular and by advice was called 'The Western'. A saloon themed bar with a little dance floor in the city of Wiesbaden, not too far from Mainz. The Deutsche Mark (German Currency then before the Euro) rate was fantastic at the time. $1 American dollar equaled $1.75 DM most of the time. Beer was cheap, food not expensive and not usually charged much if at all to enter clubs unless you look like you can be taken advantage of, or for just being a dick to the door man while waiting to get in. I knew this because I witnessed a soldier get thrown out on his ass by the big Turkish Bouncer and kept getting shoved to the ground every time he attempted to get up. The little pipsqueak soldier (In civilian attire) told the bouncer that he could not touch an American soldier and threatened to have it shut down and all kinds of nonsense. I agree that the bouncer went too far outside continuing with the shoving outside the club, but the guy pushed the issue too. I looked at the bouncer as we walked in, and something just told me I would read about him one day. I ended up being right down the line, later in my adventures.

It was all good, "It's All-Kung Fu". What we were doing, where we were assigned to, how we behaved to the locals, and relationships with our new command. It was getting that smooth well-greased engine and machine vibe for a while, until something or someone had to throw a wrench in it. Just like my former Police job, we had a change of command and now had a new Commanding officer (Captain) and a new 1st Lieutenant. This Captain looked like Howard Stern with a military haircut and without sunglass but wore clear nerd horn rimmed ones. Same turkey looking face and neck. If a runny nose had a face, this was it. He did his acceptance speech with a totally rehearsed cheesy metaphor filled fantasy of how he envisions us working together for successful accomplishments. He also had a routine and habit of finishing each closing before dismissing us with a question. "Is there any Rumor Control that needs addressing, does anybody have any questions of me?" this will play out later in a funny way…so stand by for that.

There were certain goals I set for myself during this deployment, that would be 3 years and some change all together and as it turned out. One, was going to our squad leader first to follow the chain of command and put in for my promotion to E3 (Private First Class/PFC) since I had the credits and points. Two, was to buy a car so as to not rely on taxis for long trips to the clubs or wherever we wanted to go. Third was to find any great Martial Arts school that I could continue my own styles, possibly teach at, or learn new ones. But... it would not be in this order, and not as easy as one would hope or expect. After some time of working at the customs mission, I asked my immediate team leader to check with our administration specialist (Kind of like HR) that worked in our company building. To see if he has put my promotion package in, with all I handed him and pointed out in my file. I explained that it should warrant my next rank to be given, without having to go to a board. I was told it would be automatic and was overdue since Basic Training. I got an answer back after about a week that I needed an updated PT test score and firearms score. It took about two more months for the MP Company to arrange both. The Commander wanted it to be conducted at a time that we as a whole company can take the tests and update their scores. I maxed my PT test and was given the Master Fitness award which allows you to wear a patch on your PT shirt and Hoodie to show you have a maximum score in PT to be an example to others. It also gives additional promotion points in our personnel file. When the range was finally set up for us, I just scored under expert and fired at Sharpshooter level but still gave me over what I needed to assure my promotion, because I already had the time and grade, schools/training etc. which were the last requirements. Shortly after that week, we had a formation and I was called out to receive my Promotion Orders and certificate of rank, as well as being pinned with my new PFC rank. One Goal achieved, and had my eyes already set on making Sergeant before my end of service. I called home and told my family about the promotion. I then called Nereida to tell her, and then the next words would put me in shock and full of mixed emotion. She said, "That's great, we can celebrate when I get there." This is one of a few wrenches thrown into my, what was once smooth flow of existence, I was describing earlier. Everything was fine. Work, going out, off time and hanging, everything was flowing. I asked what the hell she was talking about. She told me "Your First Sergeant sent a welcome basket with flowers and stuff, we talked, and he said that we had a right to family housing in the Military Community or even on the economy off base." After a few minutes of back and forth of positives and negatives, she finally just busted out with teary talk saying that "My parents are even worse and I cannot take it anymore, please let me come and you can stay in the barracks of you don't want to live together in housing with me, but I need to get out of here, please!" I was confused, because I could believe that maybe some correspondence like Pamphlets and letters and such came in the mail to talk about rights and describe Army living, but for my First Sergeant to call or have a discussion with my wife without my knowledge and make some wishful thinking seem definite? was beyond inappropriate and inexcusable to me. He was about to know that immediately too. But..most of all, I felt hurt because if my memory serves me correctly, I did not recall her saying one time that it was because she missed me or wanted to be with me and try again. Not until later anyway, but we will get to that. The next morning, I knocked on my squad leader's door, a Staff sergeant one rank up above my team leader, because I felt he would have a better chance of getting access to the First Sergeant immediately. I didn't know him well because just like the Cpt. And Lt., he was new. I followed him downstairs to the First Sergeant's office and waited outside the door as he knocked and entered after being given permission to do so. After I heard him say PFC Devine wants to speak with you regarding some housing issue and something about his wife? Before he kept trying to explain my intentions, the First Sergeant called me in. I gave the respect of going to parade rest until he told me to be at ease and asked me what I needed from him. I said in response, (As much as I recall) "First Sergeant, what I need from you is to not have any communication with my wife and discuss possible plans of any kind until you speak to me first. All due respect, you do not know what the status between me and my wife is, and I should

DEVINE 'KUNG FU' INTERVENTION

have been asked what my plans are or at least shown what options were available, before she received a ...to be frank..inappropriate welcome basket of flowers and crap from you or the Army giving false hope of coming here like everything is fine and dandy." (Or Words to that effect). First Sergeant started with an explanation that "The United States Army has organizations such as the USO, and they are big on supporting troops in theater. We too do our part to be of service and support here too, and have members, mostly relatives of servicemen like my wife, orchestrate their own support groups and have volunteers like other spouses, who is in a group that puts together such welcome baskets with and for the Military Wives club," etc. and blah blah blah...but... as he was speaking, I was staring out the window almost totally deaf from the blood rush of fury that I had before even going in until my Squad Leader woke me from my trance yelling "Devine!..Is there something interesting outside that window, because you are starting to piss me off!" It took everything I had to not curse this poser out. I simply said, "negative SER-GEANT! In a way like his title was a joke to me by emphasizing the rank. I can hear you fine SER-GEANT! I was just thinking about what the First Sergeant was telling me SER-GEANT! But I copy and will focus my eyes forward for now on SER-GEANT! The First Sergeant told me that if he thought there was any issue or knew ahead of time, he would have had that discussion. But then he said "It would be nice to think I should come to PFC Devine, but although I am just like you...(then as he looks down at his rank left and right)...I am NOT, basically hinting that he does not answer to a low ranking puke like me. I asked permission to carry on and recall my family to discuss next steps and I will let the chain of command know what my future "living Conditions will be and where". I talked to my wife and told her everything I had to say about my feelings on it, and what happened with the meeting with the First Sergeant, but after some talk about the past and possible future, I agreed to at least bring her over and see from there where it goes. I started looking into what was available and learned there was a list, and it went not only

131

by availability, but also by Rank of who gets what as far as housing. So, until I got notification, it was still the barracks life. My next step was to get a car. A used non expensive type that could at least get me from point A to point B. There were soldiers leaving the country and hung-up fliers in the PX areas and in the cantina restaurant. I bought a Piece of shit Volkswagen Golf for $500 USD from a soldier desperate to get rid of it so he can clear easier and get the fuck back to the states. This was so used, that the engine was being held in place with a rope tied on both left and right ends to avoid it falling out or tipping too much. Another goal achieved. I was the bitch boy designated driver for the whole gang to go downtown to bars, to housing area PX shopping, to restaurants, etc. I didn't mind, at least not at first.

Now that I had a set of wheels, I went to explore where I could find a great Martial Arts school. I have met a lot of Polizei when rotating onto patrol duties with other squads to fill in and do a ride along. When I inquired about Martial Arts close by, they told me many of them are training under an Olympic level Tae Kwon Do Instructor named Andreas. Perfect to continue my training. In any free time I had during the week I would go down to his studio and be treated like royalty. I always brought a uniform and belt with me at a minimum to be a guest student or instructor and always willing to throw on a white belt again and learn another style. I was sweating like a hostage after what they consider a warmup. It was equal to many of my full classes and my legs felt like a thousand pounds each. I wasn't used to being in a open locker room with about 40 uncircumcised dicks swinging though, and I found out they had a whole sauna, steam room, and a wall with dozens of shower heads to sand under to refresh after class, so now I got it and understood why everybody was 'hanging around.' (Intended Pun) Another Goal has been reached, and I had a sense of normalcy again and the machine was running smoothly, for now.

"A goal is not always meant to be reached; it often

serves simply as something to aim at. If you spend too much time thinking about a thing, you'll never get it done."(Bruce Lee)

I had continued to frequent some clubs with a few of the soldiers I considered brothers that I graduated with. One that was on another base that had theme nights, like top level would be hip hop or club music and the other downstairs would be country I never learned country line dancing until I joined the Army and was surrounded by a lot of country fucks from all over, and I enjoyed it as well as some of the popular star's music like George Strait, and Garth Brooks. The club I mentioned earlier, 'The Western' was a dive but they did have a variety of attractive women frequently in and out. Spandex bodysuits and shorts were very popular because every other female was wearing them like they just came out. There was one German girl, sitting in the corner with a long jacket on but one leg propped up showing bare legs just letting the jacket open and falling far enough to show a little hint that she was wearing tight spandex shorts jacked up. I struck up a conversation and offered to buy her and her girlfriend a round of drinks but used the very little German chopped up with English to do so. We got a quick crash course in the language with a Head start Program before deploying. I kept it in the back of mind that most of these women are Visa hunters to find a man and get to go to the states with hopes of some life. That has not changed in decades since WWII, Vietnam, or any deployments that involve Americans occupying for a certain amount of time. Just like false promises from soldiers has not changed from giving that life and leading on these kinds of girls. I was not going to be one of those who gave false hope, and I said it up front when asked. Girl: "Are you married". Me: "Yes" Also Me: "Do I still want to fuck you, yes".. am I going to leave her for you?..No, that would be for our own reasons if we split.`` This girl who I mostly continued to meet up with, said she understood that anything we ended up doing was strictly a sexual relationship and I was not planning on anything serious or any title. Her name was Sabina. I had one soldier who hung with us and was assigned to our company but was not in my graduating class who was some Command Sergeant Major's (CSM) Kid and made that known a few times. I went to get lunch with him at a small café, and some burned out German Civilian who called himself ALF like the TV character he had a tattoo of on his arm came to us, laid a brick of hash on the table and asked us if we wanted some. This soldier, like a fucking tool, whips out his wallet with a PX bought Military Police badge pinned in it like he was an undercover Narc. I told him silently to put that shit away and the whole western town is not going to freeze by him showing that little tin. I should have known he was trouble. The friend of the one I was 'Seeing' was gorgeous, but was pregnant, as in almost full term, hidden by her long jacket until we all went out and chilled somewhere else that she took her jacket off and revealed. This one soldier I described as a CSMs son, didn't seem to mind at first about her pregnancy and hooked up with her anyway, but I guess had felt guilty and ashamed the next day. The next morning at the barracks, he made it a point to loudly yell some shit talk when another soldier asked him how the night went. This POG answered with "I had a good time with someone, but not with some asshole from Rockland County " and "You gotta watch out for those assholes from Rockland County NY", obviously meaning me. Apparently, he was talking with Sabina's friend and was told how hurt Sabina was that I was still legally married, and that she was coming to Germany and that she really liked me, but I said it was not going to be more than a sexual relationship etc. So, this hero wanted to act all gallant and stick up for her and mouth off about me but no balls enough to do it directly. I put him in his place and told him my business is none of his own and he has no idea what my status is. I also told him he is just jealous and pissed because he fucked a full-term pregnant woman and then suddenly got morals. Then some more of my so-called buddies jumped in like, "well, you can't be out there doing that, or looking at others, you are married." Like all of them are from the church or something and getting on my ass and narrating my life. So, I got so fed up with the whole subject and said, "Ok, all of you are young and have no idea what you are talking about, and you are thinking with the wrong head trying to defend my wife's honor not knowing our status. I don't need a lecture from any of you." Let me see a show of hands, since you all saw my wife at graduation." "How many of you want to fuck my wife or thought about it? "..(Every fucking hand went up without pause.) "I rest my case" "you are no different so shut the fuck up." I then turned back to this stuck up righteous POG who indirectly called me an asshole and told him anytime he is feeling froggy..JUMP. Of course, wimps like this must hide behind daddy's rank or threats of having me charged through the command. Piece of shit pussy. I heard that he went for a promotion board, or 'Soldier of the Quarter' board or something like that, and when they asked why he should be selected or promoted?..he looked at the board members (that usually consist of your own Squad leader, the Lieutenant, and maybe the commander and some other Noncommissioned officers) chuckled and said while flipping his hand over and gliding it like when you say "Smooth" then said "Because I am Squaaaared AWAY.! With that exact dragged version. They threw him out 1..2..3 and he would not be allowed to face the board for a long while. Fucking tool. Fortunate for him, it never came to a fist fight between he and I. I would have snapped that fucker in two within seconds, and it wouldn't even be a workout. I could tell that this military life was already changing my ways of thinking, after some things seen, done, and known, it was making me more callus to others, my religion, and I was not a man of peace anymore, and I really did not want to be to tell you the truth. I was in total "fuck everybody, everything, and get what I can from this deployment that was taking me away from the real world. Yes, I had that Alpha male syndrome embedded in me between being a cop, an instructor that was used to having anyone from 3 years old to senior citizen bowing to me, and now a soldier who has proven to set his goals and achieve them. I may have fallen from grace with my relationships and know that was my own doing and not just blaming time away being the enemy, apart from my wife or family, but a conscious choice taking advantage of that time and letting anything and anyone else fill that hole in my heart and body. To me, it was ok, "It's All- Kung Fu ". Understanding you have balance or lack of it in some areas in your life, doing something about it, even if mistakes or bad choices are made, it's what you learn or are willing to do about them. Who you surround yourself with and try to form better habits that create an atmosphere you can live in as yourself, not trying too hard and wasting energy by living as someone you are not.

Chapter Eight

"PARTY OVER/TESTING IN PROGRESS"

So shortly after a few more escapades on the weekends or I should say 'sex-capades,' and with some times hanging with the guys getting into a few scraps with testosterone beer filled asswipes from other units who may not like MPs or some bullshit like that, the wife finally made it over to Mainz. I had obtained a family housing unit in Martin Luther King Jr. Village, not too far of a drive to my base where my company was at. I had spent most of the prior month doing the paperwork, ordering any furniture and basic needs that were limited to whatever was allowed and available by that billeting office on the same grounds. Anything else we may need or require, would have to be bought on our own. After picking her up and going through the awkward hesitant half ass hug and welcoming, I drove her to the unit and told her to get settled and I would go take her to my company and introduce her around since I was given this day off to take care of all the transporting and moving in on that day. She recognized some of the privates I graduated with and introduced her too back then, and just introduced her to whoever had been around moving through the hall or in their office, to include the First Sergeant of course, who kept close tabs on the arrangements of her coming over and suggested getting together with the wives real soon. Then we saw the Commander, who gave a rehearsed cookie cutter and clueless praising of me and my 'Contributions' to the unit. Finally, who was left around in my chain of command was the 1st LT. who was more squared away and down to earth than all of them put together. He gave off that college boy, pre-law vibe but still had a little jock wiseass aura when he wanted to crack a joke, or poke fun.

The first week was a lot of back and forth between post duty at customs or road, getting the wife situated and ordering anything extra we were lacking, because let's face it, the housing furniture was 90% brown office looking crap from the couch to the dining room table. We also didn't trust any bedding or mattress so there went a few pay periods getting our apartment in order. With the crazy schedule between work, my Martial Arts training, and moving, I still stayed at the barracks in a room shared with another private that I could tell was anxious for me to move out, like he expected to be on his own. Very doubtful they will allow anyone of low rank to have their own room. I did invite my wife to join me and the guys a few times out to eat, and to the club in the housing grounds that had also different theme nights. One of my soldiers 'Trent, was a straight up cowboy. Rodeo, farm working hay bailing forearmed slang scrawny fucker. He wore a huge buckle with a 'T' in gold on it. He had some good quip southern sayings that came out of nowhere depending on the situation. One that sticks in my mind is when he was telling us his feelings about 'Kathy Ireland,' the famous Swimsuit model. Trent looked at me and said, "Devine, Kathy Ireland is so hot, I would carry two buckets of shit across the Mojave Desert, just to hear her fart over a radio." He was one of the privates, who ran the sexcapades in the laundry room in basic training, fucking everything willing. He would show us how to line dance or two step and define wtf 'Honky Tonkin' meant by taking his cowboy Stetson hat, tilt it down almost covering his eyes, kicking back in a chair and sipping a beer while listening to the country music and eyeball the opposite sex. I should have kept that in the back of my mind, his antics and behavior, but I was no angel either. You would figure a brother in arms is someone you could trust, so I didn't think too hard about it. Until later down the road anyway. After a while of the routine of going out together whenever free to, with or without the guys, and some outings the Commander or 1st Sergeant hosted for us to attend involving all families, I decided to move in fully with Nereida in the family housing and drive back and forth every day or to wherever I needed to go. After some more talks during the months and reminiscing of good times or plans we made, we were back to being intimate leading to the birth of my first son Michael. I gave him my middle and confirmation name, so it was Michael Joseph Devine that was put on the Birth certificate. I thought she was joking about being in labor considering it was April 1st (Fools Day), but she went from 2 to 10cm immediately, I couldn't even get a coffee while waiting, when they yanked me from the halls of the ward and into some O.R. garments to witness his birth and cut the cord. Fast forward to now as a note: My oldest son Michael is a popular singer, a tenor. I knew this would be his destination because as an infant, he had the loudest, wall shaking, glass breaking level cry to the point where my family knew exactly where we were in the airport when we took him home on leave to show him off to the family in NY, I will talk about a little later.

Back to the beginning during his infancy, Michael was a non-sleeping, colic crying ball of nerve testing anger. I am the one who ended up rocking him, feeding him, and soothing him 85% of the time because his mother has serious postpartum. I sympathized with her because there were a few times where it went on and on so bad that I wanted to put my head through a wall. I was not able to participate in my outlets for a while, like Tae Kwon Do downtown, go out to hang with the other soldiers, and just basic 'Me time'. This slowly resulted in fits and arguments with each other and resentment on both our parts. I told her I needed to do something else to get out for a bit but closer, so to be there in case she needed me. I started looking to see if there was anything available to do or participate in on the housing grounds itself that may interest me. Like it was an omen, I saw a flier advertising a Tae Kwon Do Program run by youth services. It ended up being run in the recreation building side gym area directly across the grass field behind my apartment. "How convenient is that!" I said to myself. I went on the next night that they held class, and observed a tall older gentlemen, who had the usual black V collar trimmed WTF uniform top, (World Tae Kwon Do

Federation)..not the other 'wtf,' ..lol. But..I also noticed he was quite "Robust" for being a head Instructor, but hey..I was not one to talk. I fluctuate with my weight often and for years. I watched from the sidelines, and met parents of kids participating and asked them the usual general questions of how they liked it, is he good, etc. Like I was a parent looking for a program for his own children. The instructor left the students with a kid, who had a Black Belt on to continue leading the class in some basic kicks. He came over and immediately coughed out a full resume of his degrees and titles. He introduced himself as Dr. Dave, and then it was a spewing list of academic accomplishments from there. Masters in this, PHD in that and blah bla bla, but this well-educated man ended the description of his background by telling me his master was a 9nt degree black belt. Yes, I spelled it right by how he said it, (Nine "T") instead of ninth. Just like my well-educated father who still street spoke 'Dis, Dat, and a few of Dose'. Part of his verbal resume he finished within a rolling 2 minutes nonstop, was the fact that he was fluent in German, and it gave the chance for German born students to attend too if they were part of a service member's family. Turns out his wife was the service member, and he was the civilian contractor or volunteer and the two children with black belts were his sons. His sons, one older than the other, were kind of awkward in that typical non socialized 'Flowers in the Attic' pale home-schooled for life look. The two of them looked like characters out of "Lord of the Rings' with slicked down greasy bowl cut hair and cherub type eyes and expression.

When he was finally done with his life story, I told him my background and intention. I said I have been doing Martial Arts since childhood, named my ranks and styles and said that if he could convince his Korean Masters to test me by video submission or live, for my next level, that I would assist his class voluntarily so he could concentrate on different instruction at the same time as me. One could be rotating a 'Hapkido' (Korean art of Self Defense Moves) group while the other concentrates on TKD forms, then switches and so forth. He wanted to see any documentation I had showing such a background and I could tell it was not only to assure qualifications to teach these kids, but it was an ego thing. Like a challenge, or he felt threatened with having someone more qualified coming around and trying to change anything. I told him again, I would be glad to take my "Love me Wall" full of certificates and media I have been part of, etc. But I was just interested in continuing my journey and achieving more rank and his master was qualified to do it since it was under the same Federation. Dave could not because he was not high enough in rank to promote me directly. It was obvious I had to prove myself. So, I requested all I had copies of from the states as well as whatever I had there already as far as my Rank Certs, schooling from all styles and recognitions etc. He made a recommendation letter stating all the documentation he has reviewed from me as well as assuring that I will master all the required forms and myriad to include video footage of each. It was a pain in the ass, because we only had VHS cassette capability back then unless it was photos to send to his master that he was preparing to submit this package for, when tested and completed. This would take a while and be costly, because I will say this about Tae Kwon Do and a lot of styles. That although you earn it and know all the required forms and techniques, it also comes down to money. During the years, Martial Arts has become so commercialized that testing is now in the hundreds. As many years and money, I put into my Martial Arts studies, I could buy a multi-family house and vehicles with, and this was not going to be any different. They, (The Federation under the Kukiwon Korea Government) give a big show, registration fee, testing fee, passport type of picture ID of recognition as an official black belt and degree, a certificate, and all sorts of hidden fees just to have another thing hung on my "Love Me Wall" saying I can teach or know some shit.

I was in a groove now and had set a schedule to satisfy all facets of my life. Work, the family, my training and training others, and still some time for socializing with the soldiers and going out here and there. I signed up for some more criminal justice classes held on our base through Central Texas College. I was also back in competitive mode, logging in hours of my training and teaching in the States to go for any opportunities or awards that recognize the commitment. After a few months of waiting after submission I received the USA Award by the Amateur Athletic League for Tae Kwon Do, Unfortunately, although it was submitted while President Bush (Sr.) was still in office, by the time I got it, 'Bill Clinton' was in the signature Block on the Award. I haven't hung that shit up to this day. One award that I was not aware of, was a submission by a 1st LT. who also was a black belt assisting the Youth Services Class. He had a Colonel sign off on it which gave it promotion points as an official US Army recognized award and achievement for my volunteer work. My First Sergeant had a Korean wife just like our Commander and expressed to me a kind of new respect and I could tell he must know some shit, and familiar with it, which would explain his calm low volume demeanor.

I also wanted to compete in any tournaments that may happen, whether on a US Base or on the German economy. I found out that the Military had such organizations like one being, LMARS, (Liberation of Martial Arts Society) or something like that. I had gone with Dave and his kids to compete in forms and fighting. In Ramstein Germany air base, it was open to Germans too. I set myself out to walk around and introduce myself to instructors and anyone who stood out. I do this 95% of the time for respectful and networking purposes, but if I am competing that day, and I think that they are going to be my competition, I mix a little psychological warfare in it. I would walk up to someone, maybe in the same style uniform as an example. I would introduce myself, ask how they feel that day and if they are ready. I usually get a positive response and give one right back by closing the discussion with "Well, that's good, but I plan on winning today so I will see you soon and good luck." I usually glance back over my shoulder to see their reaction and 99.9% of the time, they look worried or confused like" WTF just happened," or "What does this guy know?" which I just nod with a confident smile like "Yeah, that's right bro". I could tell this works because sure enough, when such a person is called up to meet me in the middle and start the Sparring (Kumite) or (whatever you want to call this point system rules crap,) I see the expression on their face, looking me over wondering shit like "Who is going to hit first" and once again "What does this guy know and coming with". That kind of hesitation and distraction is exactly what I implant in these guys. Once I do move, they flinch, or brace themselves for the unknown, and that is enough time for me to go for it, or even the opposite direction from what they expect, revealing to me their open spots, their weaknesses, and reaction to anything I come with, allowing me to score successfully. Does it always work, "No", but most of the time back then, "yes." I would also observe and cheer on Dave's kids, who I had no idea up to this point what their father had taught them as far weapons, because it's the first time I saw them holding a pole (Bo Staff). They did some form, and parts I could tell what was intended to be executed, failed miserably. Instead of the usual figure eight fluent rotation of the staff to confuse or power the next strike against an opponent, these two just stood there flicking the staff like a stalling propeller on a cargo plane, fanning up and down without any rotation at all. There were some thrusts, some turns and delayed unmotivated "KIAs" (Yells). Not surprisingly, the judges held up low scores for both. I was not just embarrassed for them, but heartbroken when I saw them leave with heads down like submissive beaten dogs. I had decided to set myself out to observe Dave more and the way he does his own forms. I have seen him delegate and micromanage the class but not really have I seen his ability to demonstrate. Where there is smoke, there is fire and he had to be the one responsible for this lack of technique being displayed from his two black belt sons.

It was my turn to compete in the Black Belt forms category. I decided to compete in Kung Fu style form and uniform that day because just about 90% of everybody there was Tae Kwon Do or some Karate style. I told Dave that since he didn't enter to compete, I was independent and not representing a school of any kind and was confident in my ability to take something home. If I knew his sons were going to be such a flop, I would have redeemed them by bringing my Dobak and representing Tae Kwon Do. There was only one other Kung Fu artist in the competition, and his name was 'Schumacher'. He was a wushu artist and did a very acrobatic hand sprinting, jumping, land in split or on back, long form. It looked like a figure skater mixed with a gymnast but with an excellent display of athleticism and flexibility. I beat him in forms but lost in fighting. I also was Ramstein Germany champion 2 years in a row, but that second year, I looked in the audience and saw at least a few, including 'Schumacher', that decided not to compete, but to just judge or watch their students. I know if they did compete, they could have beat me the way I was feeling that day. When we got back to teaching at Youth Services one night, I asked Dave what forms he had to do to submit for his master, in the next few months from then. He decided to jump in and test at the same time as my submission for his next dan ranking but then stop and allow me to continue with my requirements which were more than his. He showed me his version of a Second-degree Black Belt form. Full of Mountain Blocks and turns and punches. Now I understand. Every punch he made was with a big breath and shake of his face like someone doing a bad impersonation of "Nixon", his every turn was a slow bad country line dance move, and the kicks were like he stubbed his toe, or had a cramp and could not shake it out. He could not chamber or hold any kick and was merely lifting his leg to unstick his balls or something. This was the typical proof of money for rank, memorize a form and move on BS that most Martial Arts have fallen into. I checked his master's reputation by name, and he was a well-known Korean Master and headed the United Martial Arts foundation in the states and on the board of master's from Korea for the World TaeKwonDo Federation. This urged me to get all material submitted and recognized by the actual source.

It finally happened a while down the road, because upon entering the gym one night, I saw a tripod with a video camera ready and a table with papers stacked like score sheets. I saw some suits wearing Asian males with Dave with all their arms behind them while Dave was showing them around and talking. The 1st LT. that submitted the award for me and had kids in the class approached me and said this was all for me. It was my 5th dan test and that I would be doing it live in front of these masters who flew over and on tape to have records for the Grandmaster in the states to evaluate and have for his records. I was shocked. Dave reaffirmed what I was just told and said he would go first, because they only required him to show new material and forms from his last test up to that point. For me, they did not know me, and have never seen anything from me, so I had to demonstrate anything they wanted. I did every form from 'Il Jang all the way to Shipjin.' I had shown over or at least 70 different Hapkido techniques against different scenarios before they stopped me, satisfied, I guess. I sparred with whoever was willing. The last physical test was breaking. I did two dangling with a palm. 5 with a fist, and a stack of at least 5 or six with multiple angle kicks (Front, Side, Spinning heel) and elbow. I feel that although understandable, Koreans are very skeptical about making it easy for an American to achieve this rank, and when it came to the forms, they would throw a curveball like asking me "What is the purpose of that move, where did it get its name from? what is the 16th move of the form such and such..." I knew my shit well enough that I even had my own memory tricks in my head of how to remember what move, what number, odd vs. even numbers and divide the two. Don't ask me now, that would be a huge web to clear. The test was over, and I thought I would just drink some Gatorade and leave, "but wait, there is more," as the commercials say. Dave went into his bag, pulled out a gong, and a huge purple cake sized candle and placed them on the table he set in the middle after the masters were done with their note taking, scoring or doodling for all I knew. He told all to come to attention as he lit the candle and hit the Gong making it swing and project a Tibetan type of Om ring. He said:"In recognition of his time here, and throughout his life of indomitable spirit, I want to present Sa Bum Nim Terry with an official belt under our organization until he receives his Master belt from our Grandmaster after all is processed". He then went into his bag again and took out a custom made embroidered Black Belt with my full name in English and Korean underneath on one side and United Martial Arts Association in both on the other side. It was all written in purple. He had a thing about purple, and it was his favorite color. I didn't mind. About a month later, I received the official 5th dan certificate and passport type card with rank and number by the Kukiwon, and another belt with all 5 stripes and same writing but in Gold this time. There were also separate certificates with my passport photo on it that was from Dave's Grandmaster from his own Dojang recognizing my rank and covering the Hapkido and TKD. I felt great for about a minute, but quickly came to terms in the next few weeks that nothing has changed. I was already teaching, doing what I love, and already knew all these forms, techniques, and displayed them for years, just to see that someone that still could not even kick as a Green Belt get his 2nd Dan Black Belt, and thinking of his son's same lack of skills just made me feel like a fool. It was too late for Dave to change his ways and be willing to let me help sharpen his weaknesses. But..I was not going to let these kids learn the wrong way and get hurt emotionally by competing or testing and not progressing, and definitely was not going to let them hurt physically by not sparring just because this guy can't and stays away from it. This is all "Kung Fu". What you put into something. Your passion, your sacrifices to others or something, and how much you are willing to do to set goals and achieve them, whether for yourself or for others.

I started getting more assertive with Dave and made sure to

speak out a plan of action for the next few weeks. He had a habit of interrupting and trying to subliminally shush me whenever I would Instruct the class. I would verbally tell them to break up into groups and practice whatever it is I wanted them to work on and then change it up halfway into class for variety of working with different sized students, structure, different ranks and skill sets and get out of the robotic mundane TKD night of a half hour of stretching and exercise and 15 or 20 minutes of TKD and the rest usual overtalk by the instructor. It was time and money I put out into equipment I bought and brought in, but they needed contact pads, breakaway boards to build up ability and confidence, a free-standing bag to practice full contact on, focus mitts and paddles to hone in their strikes from biggest to smallest targets, and lastly, someone to call cadence with their forms by the numbers to make sure they are in unison with each other and sharp. Nobody likes to change, and I understand growing pains, but although it was not my class from the start, I was the higher rank and damn well a better instructor. I did not want to take over, but I was going to make it better and pass it on for when I would leave one day. That day came sooner than ever expected.

I was now on rotation back to doing patrol with an NCO (Non-commissioned Officer), an E6 SSG Martin, who was also very sharp at field drills we would have to occasionally hold, to stay proficient in case of deployment elsewhere. He would be one of those cliché speech givers like in a military movie by lines like "Who the hell are you talking to private? You're talking to a Non-commissioned officer of the United States Army mister!" and "We may be MPs but we are soldiers always, of the troops and for the troops, hooah?" He got pissed once when we were on a PT run and he called me out to call cadence, which I love and still in my head today when I do exercise sometimes. We got to the end near the company road where you would bring everyone to a walk-in cadence (Quick time march), so I gave the command to stop the running and start marching then did some more drill orders mixed in to direct them around the path to end up in front of our company. I then gave the order for them to march in place then halt to have them face forward on command then called the sergeant to take over to lead a cool down or whatever he wanted to do. He was furious that as a PFC I took it upon myself to take over the PT run all the way to the end and march them in instead of just calling him out to take over the cadence and leave the rest to him. I guess motivation is not always appreciated, but I ran that shit perfectly!

I would also be assigned with some of my soldiers I graduated with depending on the schedule. With the constant rotation of a mix of nights shifts, switching, day shifts, and responsibilities at the company as well, me and the wife were still on edge with each other although Michael was cute as a button, the stress of being alone to care for him was getting to be too much again for her. It was time for a break, and I requested leave to bring my newborn home for the families to see, have him Baptized, and get a recharge from nonstop work on deployment. My team leader said the commander had an issue with me taking leave. He also said that the unit received correspondence that I made the list of candidates to obtain a slot on the All-Army Tae Kwon Do Karate Team. I had put in for it a while back and planned on going to Ft. Indiantown Gap PA to train and try to make it on the team. I had the time in and saved and explained to the commander when my team leader summoned me to meet with him, that most of us went straight to deployment from basic without going home first. The captain started getting personal and said first of all at your rank I don't think you can really afford it financially with the baby and all. I told him it was taken care of by my family, and we are fine as far as finances. He said that supported his argument better, having to borrow from my family. I said it's not borrowing and again, not his concern how I get there but just need the approval so I can set a date of arrival and schedule our baby's Baptism solid. We gave a tentative date. He then jumped on the fact I was offered a possible slot on the Tae Kwon Do team for the USA. That's when all the cheese came out of him.

It went like this. "Private Devine, you didn't join the United States Army or the Military Police to just go and be on a Karate team. We need you here and I cannot afford to let one of my MPs go around the states or world or whatever they would have you do with that stuff you do. That's not your purpose. I cannot approve of you going to do that, but I will think about the leave request. My team leader asked permission for a break and to come back and that he needed to get some paperwork from the administration office on me, to check time in service and such and schedule of coverage. It was a BS excuse to get me alone in the hall. My team leader whipped out a chop and pointed his four fingers firmly at me and said, "Look Devine, you need to open your fucking mouth and say something and don't just stand there letting this guy tell you what to do with your money, your baby, and your family. Especially tell you why you joined the Army. Get back in there and fight for your earned right as a man and as a soldier, HOOAH? "..I gave a small low toned "Hooah" back and knocked on the commander's door requesting entry. My team leader and I went back in, and I reported myself once more to the commander at attention until he told me to be at ease. He said "Did we come to any solution here sergeant" speaking to my team leader instead of me directly. "Yes sir," he responded..." PFC Devine has more to say on the subject and requested to see you again so I will let PFC Devine explain himself better." I then requested permission to speak since he was adjusting his glasses to refocus on me anyway. The captain said, "Go ahead". I went on about how well off my family was, money was not an issue. I explained about the pressures with the baby getting baptized while my uncle the priest was available before he re-deploys, and we needed a break physically and mentally for all our well-being, to have that support group for us both at home for normalcy even if for a few days. I explained how much I have put in full time missions and volunteered for without compromising any task or duty asked of me and was still able to make rank, volunteer for an Army run Organization, received awards for that skillset I have, and yes, I did plan on representing

America and the United States Army at what I am good at, as an MP and as a fighter. I told him that I was in a warehouse with over 50 other MPs doing the same job, the amount of items to be inspected and cleared has drastically reduced so we end up standing around drinking strawberry milk and a poppyseed Danishes, or half chicken and seasoned fries every day to take up time. Burping and farting, telling jokes, learning dirty German jokes and curses, like the rest do every day and hardly would be a difference if one (Me) went to do something positive and successful and return to still represent. I told him I could be spared for that little while just to see if I make it at all, and it was not the Olympics. The Commander looked at my team leader, maybe expecting him to jump in and put my mouth at ease, but he didn't, he just asked me if that was all. I told him yes and that I hope he would consider everything I asked and thanked him for his time and asked permission to be dismissed. The captain let me go but held my team leader back. I was told to stand by. After about 15 more minutes, my Team Leader came out, wiped his head with his hat and put it on as he told me to step outside to talk. He told me the commander agrees to 17 days leave including travel leeway but will not sign off excusing me from the company to pursue the TKD Team and insisted I was mission essential. I was furious and crushed at my vision of raising my arms in victory wearing a team tracksuit for the USA or Army, or MPs was over. All because of a chicken necked geek who was most likely reading about Military strategy and war while real soldiers lived it, hands on, and wanted to show he had some power to flex in some capacity. That was just to be able to say, we had full strength manpower at a closing mission that would soon be going away. "Unbelievable!" I said loudly after all those thoughts that raced in my head within seconds. I guess my team leader could read my mind because he just kept saying "I know Devine, it isn't right, but at least you get to go on leave". I said," yeah that's something, at least I get away from these assholes for a bit."

I noticed the First sergeant came out at the same time I said that and turned to me with a pause wondering if I meant him included. I answered for him and lied. "Not you ,1st SGT, the assholes I came here with, I am going on leave so don't miss me too much, it's just the guys are asking for a bunch of shit for me to bring back for them". I can bullshit well and fast. I learned from the best charmers, my brothers. I went back and told the wife all that was said and done and the result. We started arranging what we were taking and a plan of what we were doing with our family when we got home. I told her not to bring much because we will most likely be bringing a lot back, I am sure the family got the baby. Basics is all we needed, and I don't have many civilian clothes and the ones at home left behind will not fit so I will shop along the way or at home. We had two or more weeks before going on leave.

One afternoon, Michael just got to sleep, after I rocked him and fed him. I told his mother to sleep when he did and just laid down. No more than a few minutes later, we were startled by the sounds of dogs, barking but also sounding vicious like they were fighting. I looked out the window and in the back field where I cut across to go teach class, there were two guys holding back their Rottweilers by their necks and chest teasing and taunting one another like two little kids in a sandbox. I got my boots on and went right out to confront them. As I was getting closer, I noticed that neither dog was on a leash so I approached slower and said, "Excuse me, can you put your dogs on their leash before I approach? They just looked at me and said, "They are fine, we got them". Losing my patience, I responded "Ok, I will ask you one more time to leash them or I will call the MPs that I know are on duty in the area, to hint that maybe I was one. I told them that there was a code enforcement of dogs not on leashes and did they want to deal with me discussing it or an MP who could make a record that maybe their command would find out about. One had the balls to say, "Fuck you, go inside". I told him you have no idea what rank you are talking to, or authority and neither do I, so that when I report to the responding MP, I will state that two males were participating in Dog fighting, let the dogs loose and woke my infant up in close proximity to where they did it and that in no way could they control the dogs if God forbid, any child was to run by them, like my students to go to the MWR (Morale Welfare and Recreation) that was there. I said to the loud mouthed one, "Don't confuse rank with my authority Jr." You understand me son?" (Typical Cheesy military line) So the louder mouthed one decided to go the last resort, desperate, no more good argument, default response of it being a racial thing, that it was because they were (what we now say African American) instead of Black. He did this desperate attempt by stating that the term I called him "Jr." and said "Son" meant to him "Boy" like calling him the "N" word. I told him the conversation is over, and they could wait for the MP on duty. I had just recently purchased a Motorola cell phone when they were made available and a sim card you must keep buying minutes on. I programmed only a few important numbers on them, and the MP station was one of them. The on-duty MP was from a different squad, but I recognized him. The two men tried jumping in to tell their story of Bullshit, but I continued to tell them start to finish about what I observed and their continued ignorance to the code. The MP told them I was right about the Dog rules, and that it was as simple as that and no need to be hostile as I had described. The big mouth said: "Well, then I want to file a complaint against this guy for racism and harassment." After hearing their philosophy of their definition of the term Jr. or Son, this MP told them that he is from the south and a Deputy Sheriff, and they use those terms all the time like they are teaching a lesson to someone and use that term to the one learning like they must be treated like a youngster that has to learn and understand. "That's exactly what they acted like and my intention" I added. The MP told us all to go our own way, and just stay away from each other but reminded these two clowns to follow the dog rules or they will be quarantined. I hoped I wouldn't have to see them again, but, just like bullies, they don't change and seem to

DEVINE 'KUNG FU' INTERVENTION

set themselves out to continue their ignorant and arrogant ways. That would prove true just a short while later, so stand by.

It was my last week of work before I was going on leave, and I wanted to see the kids in the Tae Kwon Do class one more time and remind them to work on certain stuff even when I was gone. We were in the middle of class, and then the side door to the gym opened, and two men walked in and just started telling one to go ahead and warm up with some hoop shots with a basketball he just lobbed at him, allowing it to hit the floor and distract all the students and us turning our heads. 'Guess who?' yup, the same two assholes I just dealt with about their dogs the prior week or so. Dave, even though a psychiatrist or whatever the fuck he was as well as being substandard at Martial Arts had a habit of getting personal and invading personal space while talking to someone including pointing. He immediately approached these two characters with a typical no, no, no, "My ball, you can't play with it" kind of childish tone. He told them that this gym was reserved for the class for set times strictly for this group. The two just kept playing, running in and around each other trying to continue to short hoops and then Dave yelled louder to "Get Out"...and "Leave". One guy stopped and got back in Dave's face and challenged him of the usual bully shit "What you gonna do old man" "you can use the other half of the gym, go over there and do your thing we got this side." I immediately jumped between all of them and told Dave to continue class and I knew who these guys were and dealt with them before. I told him I will again, that they are military and I as an MP, and soldiers will deal with them in my capacity. I asked the two men what rank I can address them by, for proper respect and conversation's sake. One told me he was an E5 sergeant and the other I don't remember. I told them that although Dave was defensive, he was right and that the MWR/Youth services have a contract with him for this whole area for a set time and nights. Even if we did agree to let them play, it would be too much of a distraction for an effective class between the noise and chatter. I told them this after all, for the kids and we shouldn't have them witness this petty bullshit and to respectfully watch, if they had kids that may want to join, or leave and get with the office to find out the schedule of when they can utilize it. They nodded and said, "ok cool," but of course they had to say a few more words about Dave like "Just keep that fat motherfucker in check" he doesn't get to come up to our face like dat" I just smiled and nodded like "Yeah, Yeah, gotcha." I returned to the class and Dave came up to my face and said, "I don't care who they are and if you are friends with them, I don't need that in my class." I told him, "First of all, don't get in my face. Second, they are not buddies of mine and in fact I had issues with them myself, but you cannot as a civilian, risk your class and reputation by being a bully yourself and getting in their faces. There is a way of talking to soldiers compared to your kids, Period!" I was on a roll now so there was no stopping, so I continued with everything I wanted to say. I will give the 'Reader's Digest' version with a list of shit I told him off about. I said, "Dave:

You can't teach to save your life, you can't do half the techniques you try to demonstrate, you invade personal space and are a bully most of the time when you don't agree or someone wants to speak, your own kids have obvious resentment against you by something going on because they are very submissive. You are walking resume that nobody gives a fuck about, and you lack the behavior that those degrees should show. If you cannot set the example, then just stop all this and let the LT. take over or myself, but I am going on leave and now I will think about if I am coming back to this or not." I then took off my belt, folded it once to put it over my neck, grabbed my bag and left saying "See you all later, good luck." Two days later, I found out one of the little girls in the class was playing a game in the pool with her older brother, also a student. The story was that she wanted to show how long she could hold her breath in a competition with him or something like that. She drowned and died after every attempt to revive her. I will never forget her face with the cutest smile missing some teeth and her little pig tails she loved to whip back and forth when doing a form like "You say something? take this, heeyya." Rest in Power little one.

I went back to the barracks to see the guys and hung around for a bit. Took a list of things I may be able to fit or get cheaper than them ordering and shipping. I was listening to the music Trent was playing and enjoyed Country music a little more at that time. Not the twangy, lost my dog, house, car, woman blues type, but I liked George Strait, Brooks and Dunn, and Garth Brooks the most, back then. I got a little buzzed and saw Trent put a dip in his mouth that I caught a whiff of like it was cherry or some shit. I asked if I could try it for the first time. He was like "Dan," (My given nickname from Senior Drill) you Yankee, this will put you down if you are not careful." I told him I would be fine and just need a pinch to see what it's like to be a "Country fucker like him" I pinched a little from his Skoal can between my thumb and forefinger and put it between the back of my lip and gumline but had too much saliva I guess because that shit spread open and covered my gums and teeth like coffee grounds, and some went down my throat. I gagged and spit and tried to cough the rest out. All the guys were laughing their ass off, but that was just the beginning. Although I got most of the grounds out, it was too late. A huge rush in my head came swarming in and dropped me with the biggest dizzy drunk type of spell I have ever experienced. I couldn't keep my head straight and was nauseous for another half hour or so. Trent, let me wear his Cowboy hat and I asked if I could borrow his Rodeo Buckle that had that Gold 'T' ' in the middle while I was on leave. I liked the look and after all my name began with 'T' also. He agreed, if I bring it back and to take the hat with me too for the complete look. I went to the PX next and found a Garth Brooks type of replica striped country shirt he wears and bought it. I took care of all last-minute things, and it was time to go. We had been transported by a shuttle that was taking others going on leave to the airstrip for the MAC flights (Military Air Command) that are cheaper and more available than commercial flights. Then I believe we transferred to a regular commercial light from there to NY where my family would meet us and the baby. As I talked about earlier, Michael had an incredible set of lungs. We were already stressed enough trying to handle him, baggage, the carriage, never mind trying to find our family waiting. We didn't have to, my father went ahead of the rest waiting and found us, saying it was because he could hear Michael over everything in the airport and knew it had to be him, considering I was his father and the same way when I was born.

The only event I care to mention about being on leave was the Baptism of our son Michael that we arranged at my childhood church St. Francis. My uncle Kevin, the priest, has forever been the one to conduct all marriages and Baptisms and christenings in our family. Immediate and extended. Michael gave the same hand chop sign of the cross at the same time as Uncle Kevin, imitating him as he gave the final blessing like he was saying, "Back at you Father." I also remember catching up with Uncle Kevin, giving updates on my deployment and about what's been happening, my frustrations, and the commander turning me down for the Team and almost for leave all together. Remember, my uncle was not only a priest, but an Army Col. Chaplain. I thought maybe he had some pull, and that I knew or heard at least, some commands don't fuck with the church let alone a Full Bird Army Colonel that was the uncle of the one requesting. Kevin turned down my request to get involved and told me he ruffled some feathers when he turned down a one-star General Promotion because it would have meant giving up the parish and duty he was doing at the time. He chose to remain a Colonel and stay at that rank until his retirement. I respected that and him just like he took an oath as a Paulist Priest, (Vow of poverty) that no matter how much he made, it was regulated and pretty much went to the church. He still got to be stationed and travel a lot in both capacities. I did not know until years later that he never carried a weapon even during tours in Vietnam, but walked those battlefields during incoming and firefights, just to give prayer and mass to any soldier or group he came across. There is one photo all Devines' have of him, and that is one of him giving mass to some soldiers in Vietnam around a pit, in his robes, with the rest in their greens or shirtless with minimum equipment. You can see the glow of fires in the background through the trees that were still standing. The caption engraved on the bottom of the frame read, "When we needed you Most". The story goes that minutes after Kevin walked away after finishing prayer, a majority if not all the soldiers in that picture were killed in a blast caused by an incoming mortar or such. I was also not aware until his recent funeral as I write this book, that he narrated a video consisting of his whole career mix of Army and priesthood titled "Peace" and some of the pictures have our immediate family in them but the majority is Vietnam and his descriptions of what he had faced and had to do between holding memorials in the hundreds to giving last rights as he anointed holy oils and water on tattered bodies fading away. Rest in Peace Uncle Kevin, you were the best and most generous with your time and experiences you allowed our family to share with you.

Chapter Nine

"HURRY UP AND WAIT"

Leave came and went fast, and we were back on the way to Germany. It ended up being the full 17 days with cushion time for travel included because we were held over for a bit getting the final plane ride into the Country. After signing in at the CQ office that I was officially back, I went back to our family housing unit and had a wave of total disgust come over me when the reality of me being back hit me. To start the same Groundhog Day routine of hanging in a huge warehouse with a bunch of what we used to nickname 'Herms and Gretchen Bitches.' (Herm, for Herman the German and Gretchen, I made up because I knew a German girl named that)..lol. I dreaded having to go to the company the next morning and look at the schedule and see what kind of bullshit rotation they would have me on as revenge for being gone and supposedly putting so much pressure and emptiness of an essential slot vacant, according to the captain's description of what I would leave behind if I left for too long to seek any other endeavor that he denied.

I went to the base and reported to my team leader that was hanging in his own barracks room. He told me to meet him back downstairs and that "Things changed fast" and stand by, and said, "You are not going to believe it". I waited outside and thanked any of the soldiers welcoming me back as they passed me, and some had that look like they couldn't believe I came back already, nodding in a disbelief of something that was going on until one yelled it out. "You should have stayed home Devine!" "We are out of here soon." I couldn't believe what I was hearing and all I could do was step back inside and yell my Sergeants name and tell him I needed to see him right then and there to explain what I just heard. He came downstairs and asked me what I heard. I told him "Something about us not being here long?" He told me that we were now turning everything over back to the Germans and the mission at the Depot we were doing customs at is now a "Closing mission" involving a lot of moving and destruction of anything we built and not owned or responsible for the Germans, unless they purchase it. We were to obtain about 6 different sized forklift licenses, and other vehicles used to make it a swift cleanout of anything and access control of anyone coming in to do the same. After some more details of what our mission was now, it became clear that there was no need for me to rush back from leave, give up a slot on the All Army TKD Team, or spend more earned leave time at home, just to come back and find out we are all done with working in Mainz, and all going to be reassigned elsewhere but still in Germany. This is the typical "Hurry up and Wait" bullshit that the Military has done for decades if not the whole 250 plus years.

The days went fast, and movement of all stuff inside buildings on the Depot grounds went quicker when the MWR sent people to help as well as procurement with additional bodies to claim whatever they felt can be of use, that was tagged or had a US Government property sticker on it. 95% was furniture and wall décor. The Physical Security mission we had down the street with its own QRF team was now obsolete, and that building with all the floors we would have to buff out, was now bulldozed over. We would have so much downtime, we were able to work out in a gym they had set up and were going to leave the Germans, and a cantina with plenty of food to eat during the day. We were able to just go out as needed to attend to whatever was needed without any pressure because we had the same number of MPs but fewer duties. One soldier who made specialist rank before any of us, we called 'Duke.' A typical Bodybuilder, high and tight haircut, 'Lurch' from 'The Adam's Family' voiced guy who was in a different platoon than us in Basic Training. He would try to act like a Sergeant and give little orders, or "hey you, why don't you do this or that'' to us but just stand there spitting into a cup from his dip filled lip. He may have been a specialist, but that is not the same as a sergeant or even a Corporal and nobody really put anyone in charge, so I finally said something to him and basically told him, "Why don't you get off your ass, stop hanging in the gym joking around with your clique of meatheads and do some of the work yourself." He came up to me while spitting out his chew and said "Devine, I don't know any of that bullshit you know, I only know hardcore, so if you want to challenge me in front of everyone, then we can go right here" or something to that nature. I don't remember my response, but I did not back down and most likely said "Anytime, Roid Rage ".

The mission was completed at the Depot and the Force Protection of whatever the item was we were "Protecting" down the street Another company was taking over the road unit to patrol housing and ride along with the Polizei after we are fully done but we would still have one last rotation before we fully left. We were given a time to all as a company be in formation for an update on our status. After some chatter while standing by, the commander came out with the 1st SGT and the LT. After being called to attention and all the attaboy talk from the commander about how great we are, how we did on the mission, all accomplishments, and the thank you to all, I expected news on the next units we were going to or given dates of departure and stuff like that. Instead, we learned that we would be doing back-to-back trips from Berchtesgaden to The eagles Nest, Hitlers hideout/living quarters, the bunkers, to the fields of WWII like where 'The Battles of Bastogne,' and Bulge took place, and both North and Southern areas covering the Hurtgen and Black Forests were. Then we would be participating in the famous Schutzenschnur (German Marksmanship) competition and PT (Physical test) that included a full gear, timed road march as well as a run and swimming contest. It turns out that the commander had a brother-in-law who was the German Air Force Commander or something like that and arranged everything for us to be their guests. This was like another leave for me. I of course asked if families were allowed. They answered, "Positively yes for the Berchtesgaden trip" and that we earned it. But...for the German sportsmanship contests, no, we would be going as a guest military company. So, it will be a quick stop after the first trip to drop family members and then back out for the rest. We had some time before our adventure to southern Germany and I decided for old time's sake to drive the usual gang of my wife, and 3 of the guys to the club and take some last looks and times in. We got a babysitter and went out to pick up the rest from the base in front of the company barracks. There was Trent, Jason, and Chris who had a habit of 'Borrowing' my civilian clothes since Basic, and there he was, wearing one I forgot about with splash colors on it like Brazilian Lambada days. Jason, just like the Senior Drill Instructor during basic, had a pronounced chin like 'Popeye' 'the sailor man', and even if we were inside, overcast or even night out, he had the same squinted one eye expression as he was trying to either think on something too hard, or question you, like that new police chief did to me before firing me. I was still in a bad mood from having to come back to Germany and especially now finding out we were done and no place to go yet, but at least it is a relaxed time until we find out. I was arguing with Nereida about something else, but to this day I don't know what it was, but she was upset during our trip to the club, and after I yelled some shit at her about, I looked down and caught Trent's hand reaching from the back and holding hers that she lowered down to the side of the seat with, like he was consoling her. I immediately yelled "You gotta be fucking kidding me?", you want to fuck my wife, be there for her? and you want to fuck him and let him hold your hand and comfort poor you?" then get the fuck out of my car and have a great time getting either to the club or home on your own, the two of you!" Jason and Chris had the balls to tell me to relax and Jason told me "Just get back in the car Dan" I then told them to all "get the fuck out of the car and good luck getting a ride on the Autobahn!" This is the part I mentioned earlier about being the 'Bitch boy designated driver' was going to change. After calming down a little, I got back in the car after letting them stay in the wind for a bit watching cars zip by at a minimum of 100 mph. I ordered, not asked, all to get in and that we were turning around and canceling the night unless they wanted to walk. They concurred and we went back, dropped them off and headed back to the housing unit. I intentionally stayed on the couch holding Michael until I was tired enough to put him back in the crib.

Before our trip, our team leader invited us to get together at Chi Chi's restaurant that was on the grounds where I lived. I was on duty for patrol that night on the grounds so it was convenient, and I sat with the guys for a few and told them I will have a quick bite of Chicken Nachos and then head back out on patrol. It was the same classmates like... Trent, Chris, Jason, and one I called 'Bird,' because he had a narrow landing strip of hair and would cock his neck and head like a bird when he would look around with quick flinches. I excused myself to go to the bathroom after ordering my food to make sure I was good to go with my gear on my duty belt as well as cleaning my hands for the driving wheel of that filthy MP van we drove. When I returned, I got a call on my cell phone from my wife telling me "Trent is in the hallway outside our door trying to seduce me while you are in the restaurant." He was telling her that he knew we were still fighting, and it 'aint right,' and how he would be this and that better for her and all kinds of bullshit, and to let him in. That I was busy stuffing my face at the restaurant eating and it would be ok. Like she was going to just drop her panties and want him enough to let him in and fuck in front of our infant. She told me that she didn't invite him and does not want him there and asked what she should do. I simply said, Give me one minute... I am coming." My team leader could see the steam coming from under my headgear. He didn't even ask me what's going on because he could tell by my expression and attitude. He told me to drop my duty belt and give him my weapon and said "Terry, go take care of Business but don't get in trouble, just do what you have to do." We lived on the 3rd floor if I remember. I will put it this way. Trent ended up back down on the first floor when I was done.

Enjoy that visual after knowing what just took place and how you would feel. Yeah, 'got me?'

I went back to the restaurant and got my shit back from my team leader and I told him I would be going straight to the LT. in the morning before I even think about sleeping after night shift. The next morning, when I got off duty, I told Nereida to get up, get dressed and get the baby ready to go to the company and that we are going to see the LT. regarding Trent. We got there and were invited to a closed door with the LT. I gave a background of what had transpired the night before. The LT. Like I said I think had to be Pre-Law or something, because like any prosecutor, he treated my wife like a suspect rather than a victim of harassment. He immediately asked if he did anything that led Trent to believe it was ok and invited him or the idea of anything romantic between them. If he was to ask Trent right then and there if anything she did, could be mistaken or signal a response on his behalf? I jumped in defensively for her and told him that this was all Trent and that he set himself out to hold her hand when I was fighting with her verbally and now actually set himself out practically right in front of me to seduce her, and to let him in while I was with the others. I told him, "At a minimum sir, this guy must be charged or scared about charges for sexual harassment." The LT. asked me what I did about Trent going to my living unit and talking to her through the door. I told him Trent got defensive so I "Escorted him down the stairs to the first floor and said to leave" The LT. gave a tongue to cheek look at me with a wiseass knowing more smile and said "I tell you what, you all stay away from each other and this way no charges will be brought against anybody for anything else that may be found out or reported from or about either party. "I knew our case and complaint was dead right there and then. I had a resenting anger in me and called her everything in the book inside my head. I thought back knowing she two stepped with him while 'learning' and know I caught him looking her up and down while sipping a beer afterward but didn't really read into it thinking he would go this far and act on it. But..was I really any better?. I dropped it and told her hopefully the trip will do us good. But doubtful. She made it clear she hated being a military wife.

We got to Berchtesgaden, the beautiful German town in the Bavarian Alps on the Austrian border. Hitler's retreat, 'The Eagles Nest', was south of town. There were restaurants and beer houses that had alpine views we were going to make sure we frequented. There was a museum showing documentation and chronicles of the Nazis era. Salt mines had over a 500-year history. There were ski lifts and trails, but that has never interested me. I was always hesitant on doing any other activity that may hurt my legs or feet besides Martial Arts. Unless we were told otherwise, we were pretty much on our own to do whatever we wanted but had the buddy rule. Especially if you had family with you, it was a free for any way you wanted to spend your time until maybe a special announcement may be made at dinner, or update of any kind. We took Michael down to the lobby and signed up for a tour by lift of the area, and while waiting, I approached the main desk and noticed a huge scrapbook that the hotel kept on an elaborate display desk, and it was very decorative. It had hundreds of photos, originals, of Hitler and other figures showing both scenic and war related. After a few turns of the pages, a gorgeous tan woman came from behind me and tapped me on the shoulder asking me if I knew much about the history of the hotel and where we were and small talk like that. Turns out she was the on-duty host/desk girl. I couldn't help but notice the long blonde frosted and highlighted hair that was all hers and not an extension resting gently on the silk blouse, and the skirt she wore complimented every bit of her curves, from shoulders to her tight and tanned waxed legs this woman bedazzled me. The conversation, although just a simple trivial, and innocent one, that lasted maybe 2 minutes, seemed to be a slow-motion movie to me as I took in every part of her from her lips that I drowned out the sound to focus on while she spoke, to her hands that were in sync with her talking but still elegantly rolling like a maestro of an orchestra. I woke up, with her sobering question, "Are you here with your family?", which I replied immediately to smack my self-awake, "Yes, my wife and child, but also with my military unit." This kind of admission hopefully would keep me from looking like a creep hitting on her and let her know what I did for a living to impress her at the same time. But..I knew she came across thousands like me and I was just another cheesedick passing through.

I went back to the seating area where Michael and his mom were waiting for our turn to move ahead onto the tour. There was another couple there that were very friendly and forward enough to introduce themselves since we were going to be part of the same group next to go. They had strong Hispanic accents and started speaking to Nereida in Spanish a little. Nereida understood Spanish but was not forced to speak it back by her family too much, but she was instrumental back at the Town of Wallkill Police whenever they needed a translator and the one cop they had that spoke it was off duty or not available, they would ask her to come in. I just told them, "I cannot speak it so please tell me what your names are?" (Just to break the ice and assure an English conversation so that all are comfortable.) After they introduced themselves and said they were on their 3rd child coming, I introduced myself and my wife and then our son Michael. The man smiled and chuckled and tilted his head back with a sort of pride and said, "Oh, Miguel, very good!" My wife and I looked at each other in unison with the same expression of "Uh, no..it's Michael my friend" I think his mother actually said that out loud, now that I think about it. I told them that he is half Irish on my side and Puerto Rican on her side, so I call him my little McRican. I don't think they got the joke, and were just like "ohhhh, ok." Not much else really to do except drink, eat, and look at more scenery and history but nothing really struck me as interesting, except that girl at the desk. I know, I am a dog, a child who wanted the slightest bit of attention from a female that didn't look at him with disgust or disappointment. Any chance I had, I would pass by the desk just to see her lift her head up from whatever she was doing, reading, writing or even look around and over the shoulder of a checking-in guest, to see if I would get a smile, or a wave. After about a few passes in the next day or so, I looked at her as I was going outside to see about gift shops for souvenirs. She gestured with her fingers to come over to her and as I approached, she clasped her hands with fingers interlocked and leaned forward preparing for a talk that she looked genuinely interested in starting. It was an expression on her face that matched what I felt I gave her that first day of a gentle smile while in my head I was ravaging her. Her eyes were like a cartoon where the eyelashes reached out like a finger saying, "Come here." She asked me what I was planning that day, and I told her I was going to the gift shops to have something to remember the place by. She told me that her and her girlfriends frequent this one club, and she would be there that night if I wanted to see her and could "get away for a while." I was dizzy and flattered to the point of excitement that my butterflies were full grown bats in my stomach and heart. I was in lust again, like a child. I tried to make it seem like I was still a moral man, and said "Ok, I will see, and maybe some of the guys will want to go", like I didn't want to just come alone and let it be just the two of us. She gave me her number on a piece of hotel memo pad and put it in my hand with one of those long everlasting handshakes that we all know is a Suttle supplement for 'Fucking'.'

I went to the recommended shops and bought some Eagles Nest, "I was there" mug, kind of crap, and some T-shirts with the logos or scenery of Berchtesgaden. I told Nereida that there was a club the guys told me about and (like the piece of shit I was,) I tried telling her we didn't have to go, that it's hard with the baby, and made it seem like a hard sacrifice to make. She told me to go, and it would be hard to find another to watch him and she wasn't in the mood anyway and to have fun and get a break. I showed her all the souvenirs I bought to try and compensate for me asking to go out, I threw in extra for the families too to send or bring home next time we would be in the States. I made it to the club and went by myself so as to not have any witnesses to my seeking company with another woman. Even if it was just talking and drinking, these guys would make it a whole story of an orgy. That's one thing about guys, at a certain age, we are back stabbers when it comes to pussy, jealousy, and testosterone challenge. I walked into this huge place, and it turned out 'Haddaway' was performing the popular song that just came out "What is Love, baby don't hurt me." I saw a group of girls at the side bar that took the excess flow from the main one and sure enough, even from behind, could tell it was her. That tunnel vision on her, drowned out peripheral vision of any kind and I quickly stepped toward her before anyone else could crowd and block my path to surprise her with my presence. It was a total reversal of how it played in my head of how it was going to go. I tapped her on the shoulder and expected a big warm hug and a jump up with legs wrapped around me like a scene from "An officer and a Gentleman or something. Instead, she was sipping a drink and was like "Oh hey, you made it out, good, this is a great place, and I love to come here and be with my friends," then turned back around and did the cliche girlfriend, high school hallway, "I haven't seen you forever cheer of WOOOOO!". I stood around like an idiot for a bit, then told her about an hour later that, "I didn't want to invade your space or time with her friends, so goodbye, I am leaving." She asked me if I was still staying at the hotel longer or leaving, leaving, as in back to Mainz. I told her just two more days before that would happen but cannot escape again to see her or anything else without the group. She grabbed my hand and said "Ok, let's go." I thought maybe she was going to just walk me to the door and say goodbye then rejoin her girlfriends, but she grabbed her jacket and purse and was kissing and hugging people on the way out as if she was done for the night also. She told me we would walk down to where there were shuttles to a living area where hotel staff stay and that I would go with her for a little while. I couldn't believe that this girl, totally out of my league, who blew me off pretty much the whole time I was at the club, just invited me to her place. I could tell she had a lot to drink. We got into her apartment and being the European, not body shy at all, undressed in front of me and went right to her bed and tucked under and reached her hand out in midair to join her. I stripped faster than fire spreads, and jumped in laying behind her spooning under the covers and could just start sliding in. She grabbed my hand that was caressing her, pulling her back to engage, first by the hip, and the breasts alternating with strokes coaching her to push against me. She stopped my movement and wrapped my arm around her and told me to sleep with a whining pout like it was disturbing her rest. I was crushed and so were my balls. I stroked her hair while she slept, looking at every part of what I wanted to touch, kiss, lick, and be inside of when her sheets revealed more and more as they came off during her turning. Finally, after staying awake watching this angel, she opened her eyes, caressed my face realizing I was still staring at her like the first day, and kissed me. She climbed on top, and I was already slipping inside her to where she didn't have to move. I wanted to look her in the eyes while I slowly thrusted inside, as if I wanted to engrave a memory of me that may never happen again. I wanted to feel those thighs around my cheeks as I switched pleasures to avoid it ending too soon. I had to have every taste, and feeling I could of this girl, because I knew it was going to be the first and last time for us and at that moment it was ok, and I didn't care. I felt her climbing back in shockwaves, and her walls building up squeezing my finger and tongue to explode with hard hot breath and scream of release. Then returned to be inside her returning to a slow eye matching mind-blowing passionate ending. Ok, sorry for the 1-900 sex call talk, lets carry on.

I went back to the hotel early and went straight to the room and told Nereida I stayed out all night and there was such a crowd because of the celebrity show that it took forever to get a ride back from that part of town. That we all drank too much and walked it off and was not going to wake her and Michael stumbling in and making noise, so I just hung out in the lobby hoping for some breakfast or some bullshit like that. Yes folks, the walk of shame, male version. I could make excuses and try to convince people that it was justified. Like, hey, I was only going on 25 years old, she flirted first, danced with him without you there so who knows what was said or done. You have a shaky marriage, and this is a one-time thing, what's the harm and all that garbage. No, I am man enough to admit I was a dog, who didn't deserve to be married and was not ready to, and a narcissistic asshole who selfishly set himself out to cater to his ego and see if he could still woo another female that he thought he had no chance with. I couldn't admit that back then, and just like any narcissist, I lied, made her seem like she was crazy for any suggestion of infidelity, used her trust issues she always had, just like back with the Police Roster of female names. I went against everything I used to preach against. I was not interested in finding religion again, or counseling or anything else to face my guilt until later in life. I just wanted that butterfly feeling again of turning someone else's head and them turning mine.

"What is a lie? It is to say what is real is not real. It is to deny the existence of what exists. (Peter Nivio Zarlenga)

A Biological Anthropologist named Helen Fisher, states how we can love someone and stay with someone but still cheat. That its possible to feel a deep attachment to a long-term partner (The kind you have kids with) at the same time you feel intense romantic love toward someone else and even also feel sexual attraction toward another person. That it is possible to even love more than one person at the same time because the three 'brain systems' of sex drive, romantic love, and attachment aren't always attached to each other and not always found in one partner. This is not to excuse the behavior or give any kind of justification to repeat the behavior, but just research I have done on the subject because as they say, if we do not learn from history, it's bound to repeat itself. Which it has, as you will find out more in detail later in my path.

A bunch of the guys said there was white water rafting to go down the river, and a safety class and demo was shortly going to start if we jumped on the next available ride to the site. Some mothers we knew stayed behind, but I convinced Nereida to leave Michael in their care when they offered so we could try to do something together and have fun, and maybe get my mind 'Off Things'. We got to a site, like a big camp and park along a body of very fast-moving river, or stream but wide and full of high rocks. We got a quick demonstration on how to plant our feet inside for good bracing, how to row for different directions or turns, and what to do in case we fell out or over, by laying back head up arms folded to allow us to float enough and let the flow of the river do the rest, until we could get to a safe spot to get to and attempt to recover from the water. I had some of my regular crew I hung with in the same raft, as well as my wife, and maybe an assistant to the lead guide. This fucker at one point, thought it was cool to have us row fast, head towards one of the big protruding pointy boulder rocks sticking out of the river, pull and lean back causing the raft to bump and climb it taking advantage of the slippery bottom and raising us up like the Titanic before it sunk or snapped. We all let out a big WOOOH! And we slid right back down after a second or two pause but the water spun the raft really quick and out went one or two people including Nereida, who I scanned for immediately but couldn't see where she was right away. After a few seconds but what felt like forever, she came back up to the surface in total panic mode and all training of how to lay back went out the window. So, da da da daaaaaa, I went diving off the raft and heading toward her. I grabbed her by the back of her life vest and yelled for her to lay back with me and let herself float and flow just as taught. We made it down a way before everyone on the raft leaned over attempting to lift us back on. I got her on first and I was exhausted to where they had to do all the work liftin my waterlogged ass on. I comforted Nereida for the first time in a while with real sympathy and concern. I don't know how my life would have turned out if I ended up being a single dad that day. Morbid or not to think about, that shit was close and hit home. I saw that little girl come out inside her, in sheer terror for her life, just like my little Tae Kwon Do student, who looked like she would have passed as our daughter, and I was willing to give up mine in a second to assure Michael still had a mother.

"We must look at ourselves over and over again in order to learn to love, to discover what has kept our hearts closed, and what it means to allow our hearts to open." (Jack Kornfield)

I traveled back with the group and family, playing the role of a good dad and trying husband. I did not have to worry about anyone mentioning anything regarding my encounter, because I was alone, and most knew about the turmoil caused between my wife and Trent, its subject in nature and knew better than to talk to her about anything, maybe fearing reprisal. We got back to the company and then drove from there back to our housing. I heard a song from Ozzy, called "Mama I'm coming home", and I just started getting restless and sad out of nowhere. I went to the PX and bought the whole CD, bought a huge CD playing radio boom box type, but would repeat that song back-to-back behind closed doors a thousand times. Something between the lyrics and beat soared through my heart and mind about the girl in Berchtesgaden that I thought was one and done. I was obsessed, addicted, and ready to drop everything I had just to see her again. It was not right but I didn't care and cried on it back at the barracks when I found a room alone to be in helping get gear ready for our trip to the German forces base where we would do that Iron man shit, I talked about. This is the first time by the way that I am confessing any of this in writing or at all to anyone that is not my psychologist or psychiatrist. Like I said, different times and frame of mind back then. I bought a lot of phone cards just so I could call the girl on my mind, who's face, body and smell I could not get out of my system, who was nothing short of infatuation to me. I got a hold of her as much as possible before having to leave with a group who would hear me and know it's not my wife I was talking to. She was very short, cold even. She would just listen to anything I tried to make small talk with and with no real feedback, just give a little chuckle and say 'Tschuss' (Sound like .'choose'..Goodbye shortcut slang in German) but she would drag it a little like 'chooooose'. I felt rejected, which I did not handle well for years. I couldn't stand being alone ever, or lose a partner for any reason, mine or their doing. Now I saw that I had no choice but to get over her, and if she did reach out then that would be one thing, but she never did, it was all a one-way communication attempt and I can tell it was a role reversal of me being the "One and done" for her.

So, after another week of preparation and making sure that all is taken care of at home, I set out with the company to travel with the rest of the soldiers to tour the battleFields of WWII and other sites as well as participate in some fun events. What was supposed to be immediate departure ended up being another two weeks of 'Hurry up and wait' but we were finally on the way. We started with meeting a Mr. Larossi of his own tour business in his namesake', who was also a good artist and had hand painted everything related from German Panzer tanks to villages that were war-torn in their scenery. I had bought one that had a limited-edition number but misplaced it during the years. I will spare the time it would take to describe all the scenery and battlefields and history lessons that you can cover from watching 'Patton" to "Band of Brothers" these days. Every part of the Battles the Bulge from Luxemburg and Bastogne, to include Patton's grave in Luxembourg American cemetery. We visited the 'Nuts" bar and the museums covering history of WWII with actual items salvaged. There was also a 101st Airborne Museum. Ardennes, Luxemburg, Belgium, Brussels, I couldn't tell what side of the map we were on next with so much or what was in the same area as what, but it was worth it. Stories about how the Germans were just like us in the end, that could sit down, have a smoke and a meal in peace with us, usually insisted by any elder woman, having enough of the fighting and stepping in between them, on her land or house that caught the two meeting in the middle. Kind of depicted in the series of Band of Brothers. Most were the same, kids that just got the call to duty for their land and they got that. We slept on some of the fields, and it made your imagination take its own tour of what took place and the amount of death.

Chapter Ten

"THEM AND US"

We wrapped up the Battle tours and now we're headed for the German Air base the commander spoke of to participate in kind of a mix of Army PT test and an Iron Man friendly competition. We got to their base, and for the life of me I could not tell you where. I didn't bother going back 30 years of research to find the name of a base that most likely has been closed or taken over by another entity. We were given the whole floor of barracks and there was plenty of room on the second floor for all of us. There was a large open room like a cleared-out cafeteria with wooden barrels that we were later told was full of everything from wine, whiskey, dark beer, light beer, Pils, Weisse, Lagers...etc. There were long tables that we could sit at right next to our host counterparts and enjoy schnitzels, wursts, dumplings and kraut. They also had a kind of raw chopped meat in the middle some just picked at with their hands sharing the mountain of uncooked brain looking bloody balls. My mother used to do that shit in front of me, take a piece of raw chopped meat she was making meatballs with, throw some salt on it and pop it in her mouth. I stayed away from the festivities as far as drinking too much and not eating the raw meat. I knew we had a full day of events between shooting and the physical tests the very next morning. I decided to rest in my bunk and listen to anything I brought with me and of course contacted the family to update them on my status. The next morning came, and we all went downstairs and filtered into the same open room that had all the food and alcohol arsenal in it the prior night. I noticed that they had the metal containers that we usually have at ranges to eat in the field propped up on the tables and paper plates next to them. There were eggs, leftover wurst and sausages, and breads galore as well as pastries. I loved strawberry milk, but they only had white and warm containers of milk.

After we formed up and listened to a mix of German and USA commanders voicing their piece, and usual welcoming, a brief on safety, events taking place and the order of them were given. We would be a combined unit, Germans and Americans, Them and Us, competing at the same time, not separately or one on one. It will be for time in the physical part, but the shooting will be a Better Total Score wins the prize and it qualifies us to wear the German Marksmanship cord and medal as well as the PT one, when orders are generated and issued to each individual soldier who earns them. The catch here with the shooting competition, is that we had to use their weapons, the German G36 rifle at that time. The only shot I missed totally, was my first one not knowing what recoil it would have and took me by surprise. I earned the award in Silver. After the shooting was completed, it was time for pushups, sit-ups, and a two mile run timed in our US Army way. I was Master Fitness qualified and had to prove I earned it or I would be ashamed if I didn't max it again. I scored high but did not max the run and not at the same Master level, but it doesn't strip you of the award earned. Last event for that day, and new to us, was the swimming race, which consisted of completing laps back and forth three times against the Germans for time like a relay race without a pole to hand off. That water made me feel like my legs and arms were one thousand pounds each and wanted to stop many times but never quit. The next day was full gear with a rucksack march/run. I don't remember how many miles it was, maybe 7, but you could choose to do either, walk, run, skip, whatever, but it was a timed event and whatever team, USA or German had the fastest times completed, would win. It killed my legs and lower back and I swear that I am convinced to this day that I pushed running with that shit on more than any other day during basic, or war, and feel that pinch sciatica forever in my lower back. We didn't lose totally, and I think it was a one win for one loss type of deal, but I know I earned Gold in the German PT, and Silver in the Marksmanship and it just meant more bells and whistles I could wear on my dress uniform. Like an overrated Boy scout. Just when I thought ok, a draw, we all win, woooo teamwork! Good job let's go celebrate like Smurfs, the German Commander and my 1st SGT stepped up to the podium together for something else to be announced. The German Commander said, "I would like to say again, that we enjoy the physical strength displayed here today and the sharp shooting we all need as essential", but I would like to settle this tie between us with a friendly exhibition between our man and the MP man that is a Kickboxer." I spat my water out and moved forward like "What the Fuck are you talking about?" but not out loud. My 1st SGT had a smile on his face while looking at me and nodded, as if to say,"YES! That's Right Devine, you got this!" I looked at him with a sigh and was like, "C'mon' are you serious?" Every soldier was whistling and wooing like a stripper just came on stage or something. I then saw "There man". A typical Rocky 4, Dolph Lundgren, "I must break you" mused haired flat top, Ivan Putsky looking huge guy with camo pants and no shirt on looking fresh like he waited all day and did not participate in anything else. All my guys were asking if I was scared,and if I was ready?, until I just said Fuckit. I took off my shirt, my boots and met him in the middle. They gave us brand new mouthpieces and big ass 16 oz or more gloves. I told him in chopped German and English that this is for fun, and I will just do some telegraphed kicks and whatever. This motherfucker on the whistle to start, jumped up and tried superman punching my head off forcing me to quickly lean and duck one way to the point I almost had to touch the ground. I could feel and hear the wind go by my ear and heard all the audience give a big shocking ohhhhh shit! Through my mouthpiece I yelled at him, muffled but he got the gist of me telling him to "Cut the shit and take it easy or I will go hard" if he wanted. I noticed he was not letting up by his switch kick fake out stances he would keep alternating preparing for a barrage of kicks most likely, so I threw a roundhouse to his forehead with my shin and followed with a right cross to his chest, putting him down by his own hands grabbing the fist I hit him with to hold on for dear life. I told him, "No wrestling," and to "get up and continue of he has more to show, otherwise that was enough." I lowered my hand to help him up and he did the typical straight from a movie handspring off from his back to launch up onto his feet. I said, 'Great job, and that he was talented." I said, "Now let's drink and eat together like Smurfs." He looked confused at me, so I remembered in German it is pronounced Schlumpf, so I said it again in German with a hand gesture of a little man, and he busted out laughing and started repeating to his friends what I said. Now the whole team was singing the theme walk music of the Smurfs as we made it back inside to get ready for celebration. La la lalalalaaaa la la la la, laaaaa, la la lalalalaaa la la la lalaaaaa!

Got cleaned up, made my call to the family and gloated about the achievement and surprise added event with kickboxing but was also physically whipped but not tired. After a good shit shower shave session, I went downstairs to join in the festivities. There was a lot more food, and some of the same combinations but it was all great. I could never eat without drinking at the same time to wash down and clear my throat, but this time it wasn't going to be water, at least that's not what was suggested. I was immediately handed a huge mug (Stein) of beer, and it started. I had one with my meat filled bread, I had one with my cutlets and kraut, I had one with my dumplings and wurst, and I had one with my new Kickbox buddy who refilled his and mine at the same time and we toasted (Broasted in German) Bruce Lee and whoever the fuck we thought was great at Martial Arts. He asked me who I took lessons from. I told him that in Germany, I worked out with Andreas. He raised his Stein like, "Oh Yeah, I know that fuckin guy, here's to him!" and down the next fill went. My speech by now was one big vowel movement. Like if anyone asked me anything, I would say, AAA.... EEE..III... OOOHHH... UUUUU...over..lol. I don't get mean when I am drunk, which I have very few times in my life to the point I was at that night right there. I don't get all "I love you man" on anyone either, or sad even like some do. I get the Beer shits, tired and sleepy. This night was no different. I remember making it out of the room and up 3 steps to the hallway to go to the latrine (Bathroom) in the same hall not too far from the party room. There was only one stall and a sink. I sat on the toilet and of course started the runs I always get when I drink, however, I also mixed too many kinds of drinks, back-to-back between offered spirits, and beers. I was nauseous and going to vomit but could not stand up to switch over evacuations because I still had explosive runs. (Diarrhea in case you didn't get it), so, in my drunk ass state of wisdom, I thought I had enough space between my legs if I pulled Mini Me (Bald and strong) back, allowing me to vomit at the same time through the space I offered myself. SPLASH!!! All over my thighs, the floor and my pulled down pants and underwear. I turned left, I turned right, and guess what? No toilet paper and no paper towels.! I would say no shit, but yes! Shit!.. but like I said before as a commercial, wait...there is more. As if I was not already in deep shit, literally, I hear someone pounding on the stall door yelling, "Who the fuck is in there, I gotta shit," I immediately recognized that dragging lurch voice of 'Duke' the Roid Rage meathead who said he only knows hardcore. I said "It's Devine Duke"..I am sick and a mess, get me some wet towels and dry ones from somewhere, it's all over." He said, "Devine you fuckin pussy, I'll kill ya if you don't get outa there and let me in." He was now ripping the stall door open, and I told him, "Fine, let me take off my shit and use it as a rag if I can. I took off my shoes, my pants, reversed my underwear to get any dry clean part to use to wipe myself and throw to the side until I could get it. My main concern was not getting into a fight half naked with a Moose. I opened the stall door that was tilted now off the hinges a little, and Duke was gone for now. Taking my time and washing what I could in the sink, I was seeing double and told myself to just go to bed, like I could hear that Dorothy voice saying, "I wish I was home." I stepped out into the hallway with eyes closed, bunched up pants and underwear soaking with sink and shit stink, shoes in the other hand and my shirt just pulled down enough to cover the tip of mini me. I kept that voice to go to bed playing over and over and walked to where I thought my room was forgetting I was still on the first floor, and instead, I walked right back into the party with all to see me in my glory. No Shit....Yes..Shit. I think it was two of my guy's Bird and Carl, that rescued me from further embarrassment and took me swiftly to my room that had a better latrine in the hallway to get showered and put my shit (Clothes) in bags to handle the next day. I woke up fine and early and asked my German bunkmate where the laundry was, and he showed me. I took all my clothes worn the last few days and put them all together to assure not one hint of stench carried over to other items. At the breakfast table, I made sure I had just bread or pastries to absorb and stayed away from oily shit since I was still "sensitive" from my ass to my stomach. I got a bunch of slaps on the back as others filtered in as to mean, "How are we doing today hero?" The 1st SGT was already sitting with some of our hosts, and he looked at me while sipping coffee and shook his head with a making fun of kind of smile, knowing I fucked up. I heard for the umpteenth time about people talking and I finally just said, "DILLIGAS!" Out loud. It stands for "Do I Look Like I Give A Shit?" but in a nice way for all to hear and get the message that I didn't need to be teased. It was time for goodbyes and thank you and to get the fuck home. Whatever that was at this point. Of course, between Them and Us, we had to have another exchange, bilingual formation and speeches. Thank God that we didn't have to do an award ceremony until we received the actual orders that gave permission to wear them, and the actual award medals sent to the command by the Germans. It saved us from having to be in formation any longer, and not stay there another minute. At least for me that would be ideal, Mr. Poopy pants. It's all good.

"It's All-Kung Fu." Some techniques (Actions and strategies) work, some don't, even if you practice and master them, you never know what or who you are going to face, situations, challenges, and conditions you have to execute them in. You also will never know other's responses or reactions. It's all a lesson, everywhere and everyone is different in its teachings. If you lose focus, sometimes you forget where you were before.

I attempted to sleep, even faking it for most of the way back to Mainz to avoid any 'recap' talk of everything we just did, and just back to my living quarters. We didn't have to report back to the company until summoned. Cleaning of our equipment and uniforms was on us and we Policed and detailed that company up and down before we left, so no real big chores to be done unless administration staff who stayed behind had a block 'house party' of some type. But..of course I am sure whoever drags mud and is just an ignorant fucktard leaving caked boots or rucksacks out or shaking them off in the halls will be responsible for cleaning all over again. Not my problem since I live in family housing. They try to do that shit, they will have to chapter me out, because I would have some shit to say that would be considered 'unbecoming a soldier' if they made me drive all the way from my own living area just to come and clean theirs. We still had a rotation with the German Polizei and it was pretty open to whoever wanted to trade shifts or rotate the schedule in any way we wanted, but as long as there was a body to cover it. I heard about some big rumble that was supposed to happen at the Mainz Hauptbahnhof (Railway station), between the SHARPS (Skinheads Against racial Prejudice) and the SKINHEADS. I volunteered to ride along, curious to see what this was about and what the Polizei did to prepare. Riot gear? Gas, Brass Knuckles?..who knew what they did compared to other organizations? We did some surveillance of the area, looked at different cars parked that may be more than the usual in the lots and of course inside itself of the station. A small number of Gothic types started emerging from some sets of stairs and was not phased one bit of our presence. I listened to the Polizei speak to them in a warning tone and was starting to pat them down when they pushed one officer off and took off running. We caught up to them easily, and zip tied one for us to take while other units were handed two other guys. Anyone else who dispersed will be revealed later by their caught friends, during questioning. I was put in the backseat of the Polizei's car with the subject, who was at most only guilty of trespassing as far as I was concerned and maybe disorderly conduct with yelling threats and evading. He kept snorting his bloody nose and spitting against the glass divider between us and the driver and other officer in the front seat. I warned him in German and English to stop, and he just said "Fuck You" but of course with a bloody accented spitful of rebellion. The driver had enough and spoke loudly back and forth with this guy, until the officer in the front passenger seat slid the window open in the divider. Then, it was like I was having a flashback to my father having the same talent of finding his targeted child in the backseat of who misbehaved. The officer grabbed and swung this guy around while I was holding his flex cuffs tied in the back making me look like I just got tased. We got to the Polizei station, and to just give a visual note, Polizei cars were green and white. There was not one bit of white showing on the car when the driving officer took over handling the subject. The other officer looked at me and asked me in his caveman voice, "You have Problem with this? "I looked at the others again then back at him, chuckled and said, "Dude, I am a cop from NY, That was kindergarten compared to what I have seen or done." He gave me a surprisingly pleased look, put his thumb up and said, "Oh, NYPD Blue," "You like Sipowicz!..Cool!" (Excessive force innuendo). Then I excused myself to go to the bathroom and splash my face after washing my bloodied hands from wiping all that got on me.

The days were counting down, the weather was nice, and we had a relaxed routine. It was good to have back-to-back breaks and adventures. After one or two barbecues at the commanders, and the 1st sergeant quarters, we decided to invite all to the local restaurant for Yaeger schnitzel meals, drinks, and whatever was on the menu. Putting an invite out for the chain of command is kind of an unwritten protocol, but it's a toss-up if they show and feel sometimes they do not deem it appropriate to fraternize with the soldiers under them. We however were at the point where we all were in the same boat of going elsewhere and therefore that was a decision to show if they desired or 'happen by'. The LT. Showed up looking like a college student in jeans and a college type sweater with some logo on it, shortly followed by the Commander who brought his wife, who I recognized from a few occasions we came across each other at. I greeted her, and spoke some welcoming words in Japanese, Then I was interrupted by the commander, stating "Private Devine, I know some Korean, and that ain't no Korean." I excused myself from talking to her and said, "No sir, that is Japanese", I believed her to be Japanese or at least part." His wife then chimed in, and said, "My father is Japanese, and my mother is Korean side." The commander, with a raise of his eyebrows said, "I didn't know that " Ok Devine, no more speaking to my wife with that"..and laughed but I could tell he was either embarrassed, jealous, or both. With her porcelain skin and figure and height, I knew she had to be. I still snuck in a word or two just to impress her. This was the typical example of a trophy wife, I said to myself. Just like I said earlier about hotties ending up with scum-waffle assholes, this one ended up with a bookworm officer who may have had an arrangement. I don't know. The 1st SGT showed up with his wife too, but she appeared to look like 99% of the Korean population I was familiar with. I didn't even attempt to say more than hello to her after that scene with the commander, but I think I saw some giggling between the wives and a quick glimpse and smile with a hair stroke, from the commander's wife after. That gave me a visual and a 2 second wet dream... kidding.

We were finally summoned as a company to be in formation to have all updated orders, promotions, awards, and next destinations given. Some of my guys I graduated with made PFC rank, a specialist made E5 Sergeant rank and gave a goodbye speech due to being sent somewhere immediately before us, and all of us received an Army Commendation medal for our mission with Customs and the closing of the Depot. We also finally received our medals and cords with orders from the German Commander who hosted the events. There was one specialist, James, that worked in the administration office, kind of like our HR officer. He received an Army Achievement medal, which is one lower than ours and was not happy by it clearly. When the last speeches and orders were given, the Commander did his usual closing inquiry if anyone had any questions or rumor control to address. Specialist (SPC.) James, cleared his throat and said, "yes sir, is it true you bought your wife with a six pack and a BDU cap (Battle Dress Uniform hat)?" We all gasped, and some laughed uncontrollably, because I am sure the majority thought the same thing that was finally asked out loud. The captain brought all of us to attention and dismissed us and said "All accept SPC. James!". I found out later that SPC. James already had his orders and was under another command and just clearing up stuff and thought he didn't fall under this commander anymore, so I guess went for it. Apparently, there was an incident (we eventually found out about) involving SPC. James and an MP who was with another road patrol unit. SPC. James drank too much and decided to sleep in his car but made the mistake of leaving his keys in the ignition to listen to music if he wanted to. Even if the vehicle is off, it is still considered operable and therefore you can be charged with DUI/DWI although he felt he did the right thing, he was reported by this unit. Most feel this MP was just trying to make a name for themselves and could have handled it a thousand different ways, but if getting an award one lower than us was the only punishment instead of a career destroying arrest, take it you dumbass! And shut the fuck up. I never liked SPC. James, and in fact, had one tiff with him when he was questioning my background. One of my classmates, Eric, was talking to SPC. James while I was heading to the office about my last promotion packet, I mentioned earlier. SPC. James, just like the Drill sergeants did in basic, gave that non sincere, chuckling, making fun of inquiry of me being a cop before I was in the Army. He stopped talking to Eric and shushed him seeing me coming and said,"" Hol Ho Hold on Eric, then looked at me coming and said,

"Yo, Devine, you say you were a cop? why you lyin' man, you ain't no cop." I said, "Exactly, I am not one anymore, Specialist' I was once, but got in trouble, so here I am, yup..yup." He said, "Devine, why you lyin"...you lyin to me RIGHT NOW!, WHY YOU LYIN TO ME RIGHT NOW! YOU ARE LYIN!!" Screaming like a rehearsed unchanged expression on the face of Drill Sergeant wannabe infliction of his voice. Eric started laughing in disbelief and so did I. I told him there was no reason to yell, and since he is the personnel Specialist and kind of an HR, he could easily bring up my 201-file showing all background information and all achievements and credits for civilian education. I think he was a wannabe that didn't make it and attempting to be what I already was. I doubt the Commander did anything on paper about that outburst from James, and most likely had a sit down and a kiss ass "I understand, I am just like you ...but Not" from the 1st SGT. I didn't care anymore. I found out my new unit was going to be the 284th MP Company, 709th MP Battalion. Combat Support, Field, and Force protection Unit in Frankfurt Germany. HOOAH! (False motivation is better than none). This unit fell under the 18th Military Police Brigade and has engaged in multiple Operations like the Vietnam War, Operation Provide Comfort, to Desert Storm at this point in time, and would continue onto Kosovo during unrest during the Bosnian War In 1999. I would reunite with most, years later during Operation Iraqi Freedom and sport the patch again on my right shoulder (Combat Patch) as well as a few others we fought with under deployment during their time as the Brigade in headquarters, 'downrange' as we say. Later in the same week, I was told that my new platoon I would be assigned to, at my next destination, had not returned from deployment and they were not ready for me for another week or so. I had more leave saved up and knew my family was visiting Kevin in Europe somewhere soon, so I got a hold of him and found out that this religious retreat celebration of over 20,000 soldiers from around the world gathered in Lourdes, France. I went to commander and told him I would be close by, only for a week and that it is a famous Military activity and my uncle, an Army full bird Colonel Chaplain, was sponsoring me to see over 20,000 participating soldiers and I would report to my new unit from there since I already had orders, dates, destination and would send all from my quarters when cleared ahead of time to store in a Conex. He agreed since I was staying nearby and not going to the USA. I really think he agreed because like I said earlier, nobody messes with the church or high-ranking individuals, especially a Chaplain. I took Nereida and Michael and met up at a hotel my family and uncle were staying at. I wore my dress uniform with my McDonalds looking envelope style hat with insignia crest. The Lourdes and Fatima pilgrimages, are the most visited sites in the Christian world that, just like in Medjugorje Croatia/Bosnia borders, apparitions of The Holy mother have been claimed. I was not as close to my religion as I was in my youth, but still took advantage of any time spent with family and enjoyed any new experiences. Walking the streets, touring the famous sites and chapels inspired by Holy messages received (As legend had it), we would meet with hundreds of soldiers from different nations and exchange words, pins, hats, patches, coins, and whatever you had to spare or extra of. I took a picture of me in my Dress Army Greens (Class A) uniform wearing the Dress Hat of a Polish Officer that had huge black Ostrich feathers dangling down to one side, but didn't have the heart to take it, so only a picture and patch exchange. In a restaurant, a soldier from another country I cannot recall, gave me his beret in exchange for my MP crest I had extra in my bag along with a PX bought pewter style MP Badges. When I started to go outside with the family after eating, I heard a commotion behind me from where that soldier was seated. I saw two guys in the same uniform as him, poking and shoving him and repeating some words like name calling. I went back to see what was going on and one of them said, "Take out what he gave you." Reluctantly I did, and held out the beret to give it back, since that's what it seemed he wanted. He lectured me on what it took to earn that beret, the hell and pride it took to earn it, and no one should be just given it like it was nothing. I said I understood, but they said "No, take it, he told us it was an extra and not the original he earned, so it's ok, go".

The other days were filled with stories of this water blessed at the grotto, or fountains containing healing capabilities, and more messages by God through the blessed mother, of how we all need to return to our faith and repent and all that. I could just collect so much 'Mary Stuff' and bottles of Holy water. I still had a bunch at home in NY from Medjugorje that I held up in my hands during an apparition the children known in the village were having and passing on the messages from 'Holy Mary' translated. I said, "One day I am sure I will have to take a bath in this shit, at the rate my life is going." Father Kevin did not find that funny. He reminded me of the time when I was lost in the fields after coming down from Mt. Apparition, where the biggest cross was in Medjugorje, and the place that most apparitions would take place. How I was in the dark, forgetting which way to go to the village and house I was staying at with my family. By "strange chance" I happened to come across an elder woman, who spoke English and pointed the way to a path that led me directly to where I could hardly describe, then was gone when I turned around to thank her after peering down where she pointed. I guess I have experienced some unexplained forces or true warmth and comfort in God at some points in my life. "It is all Kung Fu", what you believe in or hold onto as true in one phase of your life, and then later in life, through experiences, people, and places, may start believing in another purpose, or practice.

"To stop rushing around, to sit quietly on the grass, to switch off the world and come back to the earth, to allow the eye to see a willow, a bush, a cloud, a leaf, is an unforgettable experience." (Frederick France)

There was a point in my life where I was going to prayer groups, wanting to even be a Deacon so I could still be close to my faith, "A Good Irishmen" and still have the right to be married and have kids. After past trips to Medjugorje I would come home all nostalgic and so full of peace that even if someone would bump me in a club, I would excuse myself with a Shaolin type of hand gesture and bless them and give a quick "Peace be with you my brother" and freak them out. I had a little bit of that feeling again on this trip but not into it as much as I used to be nor the desire to be, and it became that kind of feeling like when you mom would drag you to go shopping, just to be replaced by a wife doing the same in the future, where you just go through the motions and drag feet and sit somewhere until they are done being amazed at what they are looking at. I knew I was not the same peaceful man for a while, because even when we took a trip to Italy with Kevin, we went to the catacombs in Rome, where St. Francis's bones or body were laid. Kevin alerted us that someone had broken into the car and had stolen his golden church chalice, other altar items for mass and a statue or beads his late mother gave him. There was a watermelon stand a few feet away from the car, with a teen rocking back and forth looking at us nervously, and I told them all, "I bet this cocksucker knows where it all is" then went up to him and was going to pin him against the wall with my foot in his throat. Everyone tried to keep me off him, and he quickly went to a phone. My father observed a man across the street in another stand on a phone at the same time looking at the kid. Now we all know where it was stashed but of course the local Police didn't do shit but give a false promise of "Investigating the matter". Total cahoots and corruption. Anyway, it was time for this trip in Lourdes to come to an end, and onward to my new unit. I was so over the Army already but still had just under 3 more years to go of my commitment. Three long, testing years.

Chapter Eleven

"NOW YOU SEE ME, NOW YOU DON'T"

We Finally got to Frankfurt and reported into the housing/ billeting office where most families stay. It was not too far from where my new Unit was at Gibbs Kaserne. The local hospital where Michael was born, was also down the street, so that was convenient too. The funny thing about German Nurses or assistants back then, or at least the one I had anyway when I did a checkup, was the fact they treated that white lab coat as an actual outfit and had nothing but undergarments underneath, like a role-playing scene in a porn. We ended up being on the 3rd floor again and the senior ranking soldier was right below us, an E6 Staff Sergeant who had a German wife. We did not get along from day one. Nereida, like I said, was just as frustrated and so over with the Army way of life as I was. There are ordinances, rules, and regulations written about senior ranks in housing having the authority to assign chores and days of mass cleaning with the rest of the block. There are also regulations of controlling your spouse as far as behavioral conduct, none of which were going to fly with mine, and that would prove true later on. It was time to report for processing and meet my new chain of command and unit members. I was assigned to the 2nd platoon. The master Sergeant (MSGT) greeted me in the hall as I looked around kind of confused as to where I was supposed to go first. It was a multi floored building like a high school turned Army. I immediately noticed the patch on his chest pocket (This We'll Defend) that indicated he was a Drill Sergeant at one point. I am sure not too long before his assignment here, because he was still all starched and squared away in appearance, and demeanor for being a combat support unit. He was also tabbed out with

Airborne, Air Assault and Ranger on his chest and shoulder too. I guess he was not always an MP, or not one at all and just assigned. The 1st SGT was a total 180-degree turn, from my last and was a no-nonsense straight talker who I don't believe I ever saw smile or not have a fit, curse rant the whole time I was assigned to the unit. There were multiple Sergeants that had their own duties between Administration, Armory, Supply, and Medical. We really didn't have any Garrison duties like a road unit doing Law and Order too much, but we were responsible for Force Protection/Physical Security of facilities like the Abrams Building and the Generals' living quarters. I was told that most of the unit returned recently from deployment or some field assignments and I would be doing some busy work with them until I get rotated on the schedule for a regular daily assignment such as Force protection at Abrams. I would introduce myself as I hung around, unloading vehicles, footlockers, and any equipment from the trucks and into the Conex or supply room.

Fast Forward: While shopping for needs with my wife, I went with her to their equivalent of an ATM machine. A van pulled up and my team leader jumped out and told me they were trying to reach me everywhere. We were officially on lockdown and alert for deployment to Rwanda. Just like in the beginning, I will not divulge stories, context, details, stories, or politics involved with this, and just leave it at the fact we eventually 'Stood Down'. I attempted to speak with my wife who I had to leave and not call or see until it was over. I made one attempt to call her, got caught, and the Master Sergeant smacked the phone out of my hands and threatened to charge me. What I can talk about is the exercises and drills and preparations we made, before any deployment. Sometimes we would be put on patrol, or rover of the housing and PX area. It was the policy of the stores, that even though food stuffs were wrapped in plastic, or canned, if they got wet or the plastic ripped in any way and the cardboard box it is in is water damaged, they would have to toss it. Since we were preparing to go to a hell hole that had a lack of food and was a hygiene nightmare, we would go dumpster diving for those pallets full of cup of soups', canned goods, anything edible that had not perished, to pack our footlockers with. I had two lockers full of soups for my mouth, and baby wipes for my ass. I invested in Cholera straws, filters, iodine and charcoal water sanitation items in case we were not issued enough. The company had scenarios of humanitarian relief, crowd control, medical aid etc. on an all-day type of drill they would video footage of to show us later and see where we were successful and where we fell short. I remember playing a villager that was trying to figure out some supplies I had taken or handed, I forget. I let out Chewbacca noises from Star Wars to substitute my lack of Kinyarwanda or French. I looked and sounded like a wounded ape who shit himself when they showed my acting skills. I didn't mind the field too much, but it is still something that you really must adjust to unless you were brought up in a certain way that you adapted to it faster or it was second nature for some depending on upbringing. I remember being out in Grafenwöhr, where most drills and field exercises are conducted. I called it God's practice field, because you would be standing in sunshine while at the same time see rain in another area or even snow all at the same time, like those characters from a Christmas show (Heat and Freeze Misers) were fighting with Mother Nature refereeing. One night, I was getting some kindle to make a pit fire with one of the guys when suddenly we just heard some grunting and a dark figure moving around. I put on my night vision goggles and there was a small but angry boar headed right for my legs swaying back and forth like a shark and fast. I ran like hell and jumped up on the HMMWV closest to me and Bang! that shit rammed it and took off. We also had participated in Reforger exercises/campaigns held by NATO (that were held annually to assure readiness to quickly deploy. I remember I had been assigned as a 60 Gunner, then was handling a MK19 when some joker came by driving an open jeep and aimed a laser type gun at me and set off my MILES gear (Multiple Integrated Laser Engagement System), I was wearing then took off. He was not part of the Opposing force (OPFOR) or dressed like it but obviously was some authority like a range officer who felt I should be dead after I had a little MILES firefight earlier. The same guy pulled up, but was wearing a Balaclava mask (Ski/Ninja type) and so was I. He asked, "Hey, you know where I could find a crazy 'sumbitch' named Devine around here?" I knew the voice and could not place it, so I asked, "who's asking" not seeing rank right away but it was wet, muddy and cold out, so he wore a Gore Tex waterproof everything. He pulled down his mask and I couldn't believe my eyes, it was my senior Drill Instructor from basic, so I pulled down my mask and said, "Hey are you crazy or whuut?"..just like he did all the time back then. He was so shocked it was me he took a fast step forward toward my vehicle to try to reach for my hand and whoopsie daisy!! He slipped and like a Tom and Jerry cartoon, full body airborne plant on his back with a huge OHHH SHIT!, I tried to climb down but he recovered fast and we shook hands and caught up. That pronounced chin was now red as fuck and snot was all over his mask. It was great to see him outside the whole Drill mode and in normal, well, Army normal life. I told him all about my first unit on deployment, the guys from Basic and what they did, or where they are now, who got in trouble, who got pussy whipped, who got a Gretchen Visa seeker and married now, etc. He asked about where I was now and said it was a good thing to be familiar with the field as well as Garrison duties. I didn't mind it but was not jealous of those who did it full time like infantry.

Getting back to a normal schedule eventually happened, and as I did have consistency with working Security at the Abrams building inside or even at a booth, I decided to look into continuing my outlet, and either start or participate in any Youth Services Martial Arts Program they may have in our housing area. There was a program, but the instructor's service time was over, and he literally just left as I moved in. I made fliers and business cards with my German Phone number on them because there was a lack of students. I decided not to limit the class to just one style, but to combine all I have studied and run it as a Self Defense class. I made up a level/rank system so parents can watch the kid's progress. If any parent wanted the child to continue in TKD, I could accommodate when time allowed. I wanted to recognize those who were the highest rank by the last instructor, and identified two, a brother and sister who made red belt and would be a great tool to use for assisting or even taking over if I ever had been engaged elsewhere. I also identified one of my fellow MPs, who came forward and told me he was very much into stick fighting and took my invitation to come and demonstrate to show how anything you can pick up to defend yourself used the same concepts. He was a very humble, but talented high-level practitioner. The speed and flow with any stick or knife in his hand was a blur when executed full speed. I knew I had to study under him and take advantage of it while we were in the same unit. Just like I always do, I order any equipment that I feel we need to have a productive class and then leave it to pass on and pay it forward to keep the class going even if I left one day. I bought practice sticks, foam ones, pads, free standing heavy bags, paddles to hit, focus mitts, the works all over again. If people wanted to "Donate", it would be for that purpose and not for my pockets.

The housing was in an open base type of status. Some service members were married to German nationals, and we also fell under their laws and property in some respects. I had some German students who were family members and allowed to attend my class. I knew enough of the language to squeeze by, but it really was not an issue. Nereida had been talking to some other mothers who told her about becoming a Certified Child Care Provider and the courses and myriad to follow to do so. It would be some extra money around and keep her busy while I worked so she wouldn't go stir crazy alone with Michael, stuck inside. There was a whole list of things to get and do to make the apartment childproof and safe to pass inspection by the board that would oversee her certification. We bought everything from rubber guards for sharp corners to be safe, plastic plug in covers for electric sockets to be childproof, games and crafts for age-appropriate projects, and everything else on the list. We checked out at the register and were about to leave, when we almost ran into a couple coming inside holding a young child who Michael caught an eye of also. We gave mutual smiles of being parents with young ones and admired each other's for a few seconds, but I noticed the husband did all the talking while his wife just stood there and stared more at me, than she did our child, and the aroma of vanilla was very apparent, like she drowned herself in it. She had a very distinct European look I was getting accustomed to seeing during my time in Germany. We excused ourselves and left after wishing them a good day. I would never know until later in the months to come, that the meeting of these two, would start a chain of events that you would usually see, only in a movie.

The apartment was set up, and Nereida completed her courses from CPR to Child development passing the test as well as inspection. We proudly hung up the Certified Child Care Provider Certificate required to be displayed, as well as anything else around the apartment that had to be clearly marked., like the location of the fire extinguisher and first aid kit as examples. One of my sergeants who was the Desk Officer while on Duty at the Abrams detail, had a young son around Michaels age if not a little older. Michael was walking at this point, and I already had him imitating me doing Martial Arts, but in a playful game-like way like rolling and jumping and a few punches and kicks while dancing. The kid was really skinny and looked like Macaulay Culkin from the 'Home Alone' movies, but always had a puss on his face like he shit himself, or about to cry. It drove me up the wall of how this kid would just not change his expression. Just like when you see a guy, and don't even have to hear him speak, and you just know he is an asshole...and end up right? That's how I feel about some kids. You just look at some and already want to smack them, then send them home or to bed. I guess

Michael felt the same way even as a toddler, because there were two occasions when the sergeant picked up his son and found little marks on his face. One was a small footprint, and the other a handprint like Michael kicked and slapped him. I am not saying I high fived Michael or condoned it, but we didn't have a 'Chucky Doll' to blame, and he nodded yes when asked if he did it, so what could I do except apologize for him and promise to teach him better.

If the sergeant was even thinking of getting wise, or personal, I was ready to bring up the fact that his son was so mal-nourished looking, and skinny, you could practically see all his bones. I know this because he would play in the little swimming pool on the deck with Michael. Concerned, I asked his dad as a general inquiry about his build, and he told me he was like that too when he was a kid, but I didn't believe it. A regular group of 4 or 5 max, was a full-time gig for Nereida and it was also great for Michael to socialize and get used to different friends who are learning at the same time as him or from him if younger.

I continued to hang posters up with my card for the MWR/Self Defense Classes around the PX area. It was also one of the areas we had static security duty and I would sneak a few up while on duty that may have been taken down. One day while on duty there, I caught a whiff of vanilla perfume strongly blowing in the wind. I looked around and sure enough, there was that woman I met with her husband at the PX that time who drowned herself in it. She was parked in a slot that was diagonal from my perspective, so it allowed me to see her clearly in the driver's seat. She smiled and waved, and said 'Hal'lo,' instead of 'hello' with a heavy German accent and just stared at me like that first day. I stayed at my post and asked if she was shopping again with her husband and she said, "No..he works here in fast food." I asked if he was American because his English was good. She said, "Yes, he former soldier," but no more, now live here." Just then he came out and I said hello and that I was not aware he was working here and a veteran. He said some shit happened and he got chaptered out and settled with her in Germany. I didn't think anything unusual about it or ask what he was chaptered out for, possibly medical? I thought because that is the most common I hear but again, didn't strike me as odd or suspicious..yet.

I noticed at the PX area, they had a car dealership with great plans for first time buyers, especially soldiers, for a vehicle. My shitmobile, I called it, was totally shot and I needed a new or used car. I got a Dodge Shadow, black with red pinstripes. It wasn't as loud, and a lot easier to drive without stalling like my last one. I also saw some great displays of family crests, swords and other items of a renaissance type theme. There was a huge Celtic Kings sword and a Conan Skull type, like a Viking warrior would have. I was allowed to make payments over time and had a personalized 'Devine' family Irish Crest and history origin scroll being made to be framed, but on order to be sent by mail to the states because they were not going to still be there when it was completed and didn't want to chance the mailing system in Germany. They were not Military, and just contractors. I brought the swords home and hid them away to assure no child would see or touch them. My first night of teaching finally came and I was anxious to see the turnout. I was hoping that word got around and that parents didn't just give up and take their kids out thinking it was totally over for them because of the last instructor leaving. Nereida showed up with Michael to watch and I saw her mingling with other moms which was good. There was one woman, 'Lyn,' (I will call her) that looked like a white female version of 'The Grinch' with the same relaxed eye, laugh lined monkey mouth and frizzy hair that surrounded her face. She was the cliché' drama queen that if you told her, you broke your nail, she would flame her eyes like she just witnessed a multiple murder and scream, "Oh My God! with an intense look every time you speak. She showed up with her husband who was a Medic I believe, a staff sergeant. Soccer mom for her kid though, calling out to him during class and cheering on. Like I said, right out of a comic book. The class went well, and I had good feedback from the parents. I assured them that I was going to be there for a while because I was new to the unit and area and didn't plan on going anywhere. That was the plan anyway. It went well for a few more weeks but then my platoon was rotated for another training field week, so I left the two top students in charge of running the class and made sure it was allowed and cleared it.

I had a female 2nd LT. in charge of our group, for this exercise we were going on and I had no problem with that. I didn't know what her background was but as a 2nd LT. We call them Butter Bars, because it is Gold and usually a fresh, right out of school clueless newbie to hands on grunt work. We also had a 1^{St} LT. who was shortly going to be promoted to captain come along and be in the HQ tent. (Headquarters) to report to during mock missions. He was also the acting commander until promoted and fully inserted in that slot. I had a squad leader that was all 100% cowboy with a heavy southern drawl. I was driving with him to do some recon (Reconnaissance) of acting opposing forces to get a (SALUTE) Size, Activity, Location, Uniforms, Training, Equipment report. He had his binoculars out and while I was driving slowly down the side of a field, I thought I heard a rumble like he burped or grunted. I continued to go forward, and he just yelled out, "Whoa! Stop the Fucking Truck, didn't you hear me say Whoa?!" I looked at him and I swear I could fry an egg on my head with the steam I built up. I said, "Sergeant, first off I am not a horse, second, you do not yell at me after all I heard was a little burp of what you may consider a word, while I am in a loud HMMWV with air blasting through the vents, and third, I don't give a fuck what rank you are, once you start cursing at me, all respect goes out the window. I am not a horse, so don't Whoa me ever again Johnny Cash!" I saw the adrenaline building up in his lip, because it was shaking, and I could tell he didn't know if he wanted to fight or cry. I didn't wait for shit he had to say and just told him I didn't hear him, and his mistake but my fault for not verifying if I heard what I thought I heard, and so, let's carry on. He said, "Devine," I don't know you, but heard some things, and I have done some Sabaki myself and thought we were about to roll right here. I looked at him like wtf you mean Sabaki? That's just movement in Japanese, like getting out of the way of an attack. and I was not impressed. I just said "Well, maybe we can move around a little sometime" since that's what that means'' Idiot. He said it like the whole western town was supposed to freeze, with background suspense music...dum dum dum duuuuuum and tumbleweed blowing by. We got the information we needed by our observations, and I was asked to report it to the HQ tent. I went and saw the 1st LT. and gave the report. He asked me to get my platoon leader, the 2nd LT and have her report to him immediately regarding another mission run with the information I gave. I found her near our vehicles looking really rough and informed her what the LT. said. She was in the middle of biting a sandwich or some shit, and with a full mouth yelled at me saying "Tell him be advised, that she is eating right now, and she will come when she is ready." I was telling myself that these two must be fucking by these childish, back and forth games, and me in the middle like a monkey or cupid. I told the 1st LT. what she said, and he told me now, to tell her "Be advised you don't advise me of anything and get to HQ Now!" I relayed the message. I don't remember much else about that week except that when we got back, the 2nd LT. was telling 1st SGT during a debrief and update on other matters that she should address the soldiers about what he was going to say. 1st SGT said, "Negative Ma'am That's Soldiers Business, you can go now" the whole platoon cheered HOOAH!. She walked out head down and crushed. The 1st SGT debriefed us on what we did good, bad, and what needed improvement. "Operational readiness is key," and all that motivated shit. He said you can't do PT and sit around like some little pig just eating chow behind a desk, then you are not setting the example and should just get an early out! Then he yelled "Stand Up Sgt. And he pointed to one of our "Robust Heavy Drop" Sergeants that I think was administration or an Armorer. 1ST SGT. Totally fat shamed him, and I felt bad because I have been there more than just a few times in my life. 1st SGT then almost had an epiphany and said to us all, "Maybe I am old fashioned and old school and could be nicer, and.... well, no,..Fuckit! I'm not sorry, fuck that. Get with it or get out. We were rolling at the self-conflict 1st SGT was having that went from enlightenment back to hard core, within 15 seconds.

Now I was back...again from another fun filled field trip. I caught up with the wife and she told me I got a few calls about the class but some hang ups too. I advertised the home phone run by German Telecom, so I would not miss any calls if I was on duty and could not use my cell on post. I found there to be a lot of adults interested in learning privately or a separate class if I could do back-to-back. I did not have enough expressing interest to run a separate adult class but I told some that if I had time and they made an appointment I would see if I was free to teach them, but..it would be paid instruction since it is my personal private time and not MWR sponsored. There was one spouse of a soldier, who thought she would be like a bad porn scene and pay me by stripping in front of me when I gave her a private lesson after her kid just went to bed after learning with her. Something strange about her body was that the top of her butt crack looked like it was stretched open and looked like she had two buttholes, like one on the lower back and her regular one, when she turned around arms up like I asked her to show me any weapons she had. I kindly turned her down and she decided to have a self-flattering chat like "Oh you know damn well what this was about, you know you want this, and my husband is gone until next week so you can have this all night every night." 'There are some people that look like they smell, right? You feel me'?, this was one of them. I was out! If the streak in my underwear after a workout had a face, it was her, but at least I was wrong about the Adam's apple...hold onto that visual.

I was now back at Abrams Building Security detail doing access control and static guard duty rotation at outside booths too.

guest houses for visiting ones during conferences and such. I was standing in a plexiglass booth and 'watching the grass grow and the Rabbits fucking as we say'. I was exhausted from all I was involved in and burning the candle at many sides as always between the family, childcare when I am off to help her, teaching, and work. I fell asleep standing for a second, just enough for my head to fall forward and crashed my helmet against the plexiglass, scaring the shit out of me. I was expecting my Desk SGT. Or someone behind the cameras came over the radio and laughed at me and asked if I was ok, ..but nothing, not even a relief. Along came a guy, walking a well-behaved trained dog. He asked my name and we discussed dogs, told him about my endeavor, days of K9, cop stuff, War crap and he was down to earth. I told him I was adjusting to field stuff but would like to get back into protection or Law Enforcement etc. I played with the dog and enjoyed the conversation and then he said, "Well, take care and be safe" I didn't ask any information but anyone there in those living quarters were above my paygrade, so it was always "Goodnight, Sir"

Even after I publicly humiliated that girl, my wife was still suspicious and accused me of more and was listening to that dried up Grinch Cunt who spends her days gossiping about who is doing what and being the advocate for all. At one point we fought so bad, I said, I may as well go fuck someone and get something out of it if I am guilty according to you anyway. I went out clubbing to get away from her with a Corporal I called 'Tippy' who had a gorgeous Latin wife, but it was weird because she had the same name as my sister, so I couldn't think of her a certain way, you know? Tippy had a side piece at this club we went to for karaoke and dancing or just to drink and blow off stream and talk shit. His side chick was a thick, spandex bodysuit that still couldn't hold in shit wearing snaggle toothed skank. I felt I deserved nights out but didn't need that crap, and if I was going to just fight at home, I was doing everyone a favor. I decided to get a Shepard and found one named 'Inka' that was already two years old and well trained. The most trouble she had was having her period. She would spot here and there. Well, one day, I decided to bathe her in a small plastic kids pool on our balcony. I wanted to empty the water little by little with one bucket at a time but didn't want to track it through the apartment to the bathroom. I looked below and people ran hoses and water was around cars so I thought I could easily dump it to the ground with one tip over slow flow and let it run into the lot. That didn't go according to plan, because the water hit the stair Sergeants balcony and flooded his German wife's plants and know I knocked something over. I could hear her yelling and I leaned over to say I was sorry. She yelled up and said, "Sorry is not going to cut it!", I told her whatever the damage, I will pay for it. The commotion of her yelling and then me, made the dog bark, Michael cry, and his mother very upset. Get this visual. I was in my shorts that got soaked just took them off, still in my underwear making a call at my little desk in the living room you can see from the apartment door, leading to the hallway. The Gretchen Bitch downstairs had the habit of taking a broomstick and start tapping our floor (Their ceiling) to tell us we are making too much noise. Like we are in the fucking 'Honeymooners' series' or something. Nereida did a whole Irish hard step and Jig when they tapped our floor. Up the stairs came the sergeant in charge of our housing stairwell. I was on the phone, so Nereida answered it, saw him and flew the door wide open where it stayed caught on our carpet, looked at me with disgust and said, "It's for you". The Staff SGT looked at me with that adrenaline lip going a thousand miles an hour and said, "Can I talk to you for a minute?". I was in my underwear only, no shirt, my fat Elvis hairy belly pouring over my cock, and I am scratching my head while on the phone trying to figure how to adjust to his request. I told him to close my door, I will get dressed and come down when I am done on the phone with work. I heard him flap his gums about the dog, the fights, the lack of respect from the wife, the water situation, the lack of me being around to help with neighborhood shit, while I was in the field. I told him, I am not in his chain of command and don't have a cushy 9-5 job and he can complain to my command that I am not around to clean stairwells or plant like his wife. I never gave a fuck about rank or authority. Ever. I was raised around them, and not impressed especially if they abused it and had nothing to do with me or my life. Two Nights later, 3am, a knock on my door waking me up from one of my neighbors telling me my car is on fire. I ran downstairs not seeing clearly over the balcony. I ran outside only to see driving away and a little blue car I knew well, with a Gretchen bitch blonde driving waving that pale anorexic arm and the faint smell of French vanilla came over the flames of my car's gas tank. They found laundry detergent mixed with fuel (Napalm) I had called CID (Criminal Investigation Division) as well as my MPs. They couldn't do shit because I did not see her directly do it, not her face head on and went by her description leaving and seeing an arm and some hair. I said I knew her vehicle by regular contact because of my program, that she didn't belong here at 3am. They took notes and said an investigation will start. They will keep her name and her husbands, as 'people of interest' if anything else occurs. I found out that night by one of them, that the husband was thrown out of the Army on some disciplinary action, and settled there with her, and he worked at Burger King or whatever the fuck it was back then. It was on, and to think that could have seriously injured a lot of people. I went to my team leader, and he went to the Master Sergeant. I was told that I had been summoned by the Colonel at Battalion level as soon as I returned to work. I went to see the Battalion Commander and reported myself as ordered. He sat back in his chair, and asked me, "PFC Devine, how does the 'Deputy Chief of Operations' in NATO Headquarters know you by first name?" I told him "I have no idea who that is sir". The Colonel smiled, stood up and brought me to a wall full of pictures and pointed to who he was talking about. "This was the General I talked about dogs with and other shit pretty bluntly when I was on grass watch and hitting my head on plexiglass sir!" He laughed and said, "Yup...you are his new driver MP! So, you have one day or so to move yourself and your family to NATO HQ in Heidelberg and from what I hear, it couldn't have happened at a better time. I will assure your clearing housing and all that bullshit is taken care of smoothly, but I suggest you get a move on now and get down there as soon as you can. I told everyone upstairs in my company who knew. I called the wife, and she freaked but was ok with it. I canceled all classes and said keep it going if you want and if allowed but I had to leave. I said give a big Fuck you to Lyn, for forcing my hand to piss off this psycho, and I was out. When I turned my equipment in and cleared, the (MSGT) had a quick huddle with some on duty MPs and whoever was around. He had the on-duty armorer come out and read something he handed him. It was "Attention to Orders" written like Ad Libs books, filling in the blanks, adding my name in, and promotion to my new rank of 'Specialist.' MSGT said I have done some great things, which I really didn't know what he was talking about, but appreciated. They felt I had the time and grade and now the position that deserved this rank.

"Now you see me, Now you Don't"

Chapter Twelve

"FLAGGED IN THE USA!"

Déjà vu, here we are again, sending all our stuff ahead of us in a truck to be stored and fit whatever we can into my now third vehicle I would own in Germany in just a couple of years, heading for my new destination. NATO headquarters to drive the Deputy Chief of Operations around to wherever he may go. This was to be a 'Secret Move' and nobody was to ever say where I was going considering the arson case involving my family and the psycho bitch, nobody could prove or willing to prove and charge her guilty. Talk about a cushy job I would have. He was a one-star (Brigadier General) at the time but was soon to be promoted to his second. Once again, we reported to billeting and already had living quarters set for us, but also once again, top floor, so more stairs to climb. I was given a day to settle and wait for word on our stored items that should have arrived the same day if not the day after. I had already put away what we were able to pack, the essentials especially for Michael. I reported to the headquarters building of USAREUR (United States Europe) to the Sergeant First Class (SFC) that was in the administration office. He was a little bald Mr. Magoo looking guy, older but fit and carried himself as a straight shooter. He would be the one to interrupt any tangent or rant you were going on and say, "What is your point?" with a 'talk to the hand' gesture to stop flapping your gums and spit out your meaning. I was brought down the hall and met a Command Sergeant Major (CSM) who was a huge African American who was tabbed out, and every other word or sentence complete was followed by "Airborne" from him. He had a deep raspy mouthful sound when he spoke, like Shaquille O'Neal. He greeted me from behind his beautifully stained desk that had a collection of memorabilia like little flags and challenge coins under the matching sized glass protector as well as many "Love Me Wall" items. From poses in pictures with high figures, to flags, and shadow boxes full of his medals and awards. I thought it looked like a mini–Presidential Oval Office until I made my way down the hall with him, to a full bird Colonels office who served directly under the General. He was a silver haired gentleman who looked like a mix of Archie Bunker and Tip O'Neill (Former Speaker of the House), but thinner. He stood up and said, "Well now, we finally got ourselves a driver, how are we doing so far?" He had a southern, Georgia or Carolinas type of drawl. He told me the General was not going to be in until the afternoon but since it was early, we would go to the mess hall and have breakfast. His office was huge but still just an adjoining type of suite to the General's office in the next room that was even bigger, custom carpeted, polished and just immaculate. Like a true leader should be in.

We all sat in the chow hall together to make small talk until I would get some in processing done and a clear idea of my duties. I ate my eggs, and just about to eat my grits. I opened a sugar packet and started sprinkling some on the grits, and the Colonel just gazed at me then at my bowl, then at me again and said, "You are a God Damn Yankee, arn't ya'?" Just like that and with that 'Foghorn Leghorn' drawl again. He said, "You about to totally desecrate that wonderful bowl of grits with shuga?". I looked confused so he threw his fork down and said, "Look Yankee, I could understand a little bit of salt, peppa, and some butta, (as he pronounced that list), but to add Shuga, is just sacrilege." I said I treated them like oatmeal, and said, "Sorry sir, I didn't know there was a protocol for grits. Like I was Joe Pesci, in 'My Cousin Vinny' being taught about grits. Who knew? I was issued the unit patches that looked cool in the OD Green version, but the colored one for the Dress Uniform had a rainbow over the flaming sword. I felt like a Tele-tubby when I had to wear it. I was introduced to the supply/maintenance guy downstairs at the motor pool where I was to keep the Generals vehicle always clean, fueled and ready to go, anytime he was to be transported. I noticed he didn't have a hard car (Bulletproof protection) like I

There was one that was before any gate, to clear people that would drive up before allowing access. I was standing guard and wiping my eyes because there was heavy pollen coming from the surrounding trees that time of season falling everywhere and covering grounds and vehicles. I heard a little honk and up drove a small car and a little wave of an arm from the driver. I couldn't see right away, but after stopping before the entrance, out of the vehicle came her, the German wife of the Veteran we met at the PX. She was alone and of course, I was once again wafting that French Vanilla smell again. She came up and had a blue Gi Top (Martial Arts Uniform Top) in her hands and said she saw my poster and she got me a gift for good luck. I couldn't believe it, not the fact she got me a gift, but that she sought me out and showed up at my work on my post, knowing where I was. The first thing I asked her was, who, what, where, when did she know and find out about me and my job? She just shrugged like oh, it's a mystery, so I took it as some MP I knew, may have thought he was doing me a favor and answered her when she inquired. I thanked her but told her it's not right being there. Sure, fucking enough, here comes a different SGT. Staff Sergeant to be exact strolling up to meet who he most likely saw on camera and had to come cockblock unnecessarily. He just looked at her, nodded hello and then looked at me and asked, "Devine, is this your wife?", I gave a direct "Hell No" she is someone I met with her kid and Husband at the PX and she was dropping off a top for me to use when I teach. She saw my MWR poster and knew I taught Self Defense and Karate. I used the opportunity to thank her and said, "Well, thank you for getting that for me, I will see you and your husband around I guess'' take care. She left and then I had to hear the whole lecture about personal guests coming on post. Fraternization, etc. I assured him there was no invite nor desire for there to be any socializing and I have no idea how the fuck she found me. He told me to squash it fast. I took a chance and went to the PX area the next day to see if her husband was working. He was walking around in the back, so I didn't want to cause a scene by approaching him about this personal shit with his wife. I went back outside and there she was waiting by her car with her arms crossed looking annoyed. I made a fast attempt to squash whatever it was she thought was going to happen by being grateful but firm. She said, "I have an instructor who has quality uniforms, and I am a Brown Belt on German Economy. I just wanted to help in your class since you allow German Students to translate or help. I felt like an idiot thinking it was more to it but still was very direct saying, "That's fine, but I cannot have anyone start rumors and it's a huge thing in the Military to have a reputation of adultery and I have been through enough shit with games." I told her where the MWR class was, and she can see if it's worth even trying to come far or at all for just a few students that are German. About another month went by with only two classes attended by her, but of course, the rumors spread, and I was even approached by the Staff Sergeant husband of the Drama Queen Lyn, who was comforting my wife during class like I was a monster for letting this girl in to help. If Nereida knew Martial Arts I would let her help too. But..this was on me all alone running this and I needed help. I cannot rely on just kids even if they are high rank. I finally had enough when it came to the rumors and had a long talk with all parents and especially the biggest gossip bitch, Lyn, bluntly and denied there being any involvement other than professional with this girl and to stop filling my wife's head with Bullshit because it was affecting us too. It was too late. I had no choice but to squash it permanently and in front of the class to prove there was nothing else. I couldn't do it on the phone, so I waited for her to show up at class. I told her that what I warned her about has happened, that my students, parents, my wife, my neighborhood, and most soldiers think you and are fucking and I cannot have that happen, so we need to say goodbye, no hard feelings and not see each other again besides around where we shop. It's not appropriate anymore. She shrugged and gave a look of hurt but nodded and said "Ok, Bye " sorry, then waved to the class and left.

I was posted at the Generals quarters where they reside and have had seen other Generals have when they visited my last unit for ceremonies or important meetings. I made my way upstairs and back to the administration office to be briefed on schedules, and any helpful background I may want to educate myself on about the General, USA Europe and what they do, etc.

I heard a familiar voice echoing down the hall and a lot of "Yes Sirs" coming from responders. It was the General and he was talking to the SGM and the Colonel about where he was coming from and checking on how things were going here. I made my way down and waited outside the Colonel's office until he would give me the signal to come in for formal introductions. I was escorted into the Generals office where I came about to do a formal reporting for duty ass squeezing click heeled salute. He came around his desk to shake my hand and slapped a coin in my palm with his title and flag insignia on it. Challenge coins are great for collection but also good for when you go drinking and the one with the highest rank coin in his pocket, gets out of buying the next rounds, leaving the lowest to buy. The general looked like a combination of Bill Murray, and Kurtwood Smith from 'That 70s Show. He had a very laid-back good humor but serious demeanor at the same time about him. I did research on him to get familiar with who I would be responsible for getting from place to place safely and maybe a glimpse of the kind of man he was, but you can never truly know someone from articles, and word of mouth. You must work with them, talk with them and listen, not just hear. The General was named after his father who was also named after his great-great-great- grand uncle who was Abraham Lincoln's Quartermaster general during the Civil War and named the father architect of Arlington National Cemetery as well as 'Engineer of the Capital,' Montgomery C. Meigs. His father was also a WWII hero who died months before he was born in the first two weeks of battle. A Lieutenant Colonel, and commander of a tank battalion killed in action during the liberation of Alsace in France. He was West Point educated but a multiple scholar in history and other academic achievements and leadership roles all the way up to (then recent) Desert Storm.

The general told me candidly that he really didn't need a driver, and that he felt bad seeing me standing in a booth, talking with him about the dogs, which led to a little talk of my background and endeavors. He said he wanted to do me a favor and get me out of that for a bit and try a new detail since I have dabbled in everything an MP could already. He told me that 90% of the time he uses a chopper or other means not requiring being driven and that I would have a lot of time on my hands but to be around in case plans change and have the vehicle operable and ready at a moment's notice. I spent a lot of time in the gym keeping up with my Martial Arts and strength training. The general walked in once while I was hitting the bag with some Muay Thai and then watched me doing a Kung Fu Form and said that he was too old for that stuff but may want to learn some Tai Chi. I offered to show a slower version of all I knew, but he declined. A few months into the job, I was asked to follow the general into a war room type of conference and held some materials he handed me. Not like a briefcase handcuffed to my wrist or something like that, but apparently important enough for me to be asked to handle it. I cannot and will not divulge any plans or orders given that day. No matter if it is all known and in the past. I will do that out of respect for the integrity and privacy of those who were in attendance. It did raise my eyebrows and take a deep breath to be around some powerful decision makers that can be "Influential" in world changing events.

A while further down the road, not much busy work was to be done, and the General said we were going to attend 'Operation Atlantic Resolve.' Like the Reforger exercises I described earlier in my journey. The USAREUR has led the Department of Defense's Atlantic Resolve land efforts. Atlantic Resolve provides rotational deployments of combat credible forces to Europe to show its commitment to NATO while building readiness, enhancing deterrence, increasing interoperability and enhancing the bonds between ally and partner militaries. Up to 7,000 soldiers and 4 rotations. I would escort him around by vehicle and by foot to greet soldiers, other officers, or observe operations as they were being conducted and in play. However, the General had me stay with on duty MPs that were providing physical security and force protection. They had their own cot filled with a huge tent area. In fact one night, after escorting the general to his quarters, his sense of humor took over and he felt relaxed enough to say this Verbatim, "Terry, I am going to go inside, take a nice hot shower, and let the hot water and soap run down the crack of my ass and then go to my soft bed and sleep, how does that sound to you?"..I looked at him and said "It sounds like you had a long day and you are very tired, so I guess you better get to it". I also said, "But..since you wanted to get an early start and to save time, I know you have a guest room up in there, and it would be easier to just get up and go instead of me driving back, be in a tent in the dark, getting up in a few hours just to come back and get you. So, I could stay if you have that room." General Meigs looked at me, rolled his eyes with an "Oh brother look" and said "See you in the morning Terry, goodnight" leaving me hanging and to go be a soldier and sleep with the rest. Now I know he was baiting me into being jealous of his cushy room. Good one sir.

I called home when I could, but I also found strange, restricted number blank message screens, left on my cell and sim card storage since it was getting full. I didn't get it and thought maybe I was out of range, and it couldn't get through, with jammers on during exercises or some shit. Nereida said it wasn't her and would wait for my call, not make calls to me in case I was around the general and important shit going on. The operation ended and we were back at HQ. that same week. The only other time I really had to drive long or really at all, was when there was a dedication and award ceremony celebrating the General's father. A Platz area was to be named after his dad, and he was to attend. I was in the gym when I got the call that the weather was going to get worse, and he needed to be in Frankfurt ASAP. Last minute change of plans from flying to driving. I had no maps ready with routes plotted or researched, and no GPS was available back then like there is now. The General hopped in with another high ranking general with his team, and I was to drive his wife and a guest to the ceremony. I had no choice but to ask his wife to navigate and tell me where to go since I didn't have electronic plotting ahead of time or could read the map while driving. We eventually got there on time, the ceremony took place and we returned to his office after dropping his wife and guest off. I followed him up to his office and he threw his hat down and put his hands on his hips and said "Terry, you are not a good driver, not today anyway. You had a lot of time to plan for such instances when weather does not permit me to fly, and you did not execute any plan. You had to have the ladies give you directions and still just made it.?" I don't know what to do at this point and maybe you need to get with the PSD team and get maps and routes and maybe work with them until you have another mission or something.`` I apologized and told him I would be more prepared from that point on, and he just wiped his head a little bit in thought, and said, "Alright" but it was with a hand gesture of "Oh well, we will see, "and then said, "that's all."

"By failing to prepare, you are preparing to fail." (Benjamin Franklin)

I called my wife and briefed her on the whole thing and how disappointed the General was, and how I was in myself for not being up to par as a driver. I just made it into our family housing, and to our parking area. We had assigned spots for our apartment numbers, but someone was in my space. They started backing out and then, I saw them, the two that made my heart drop into my stomach then back up to my chest. It was a psycho arson bitch with her loser has-been husband and their kid in the back. Not only were they able to find me, but to my actual parking space? That was some sneaky shit. He must have done a post locator check on me or someone blabbed from my former company that she hit on or something. I have now been away for a little over a year. I was about to pull them out of the vehicle and onto the floor, until I realized that this bitch had a satisfying smile and calm on her face, like they just did something and were leaving. I tanked again and my stomach churned with a visual of my wife and child possibly hanging bloody like you hear urban legend stories about on a curtain rod. I parked and ran up the stairs faster than any PT test I ever took and blasted in the apartment, scaring the two of them. Nereida asked me what was wrong, so I opened the curtain showing the parking area and said, "Guess who's back?". They were still there, looking up now and giving a wiseass smirk and wave. I called the MP station and CID, identified myself as the Generals driver, the background on these two from Frankfurt, the arson investigation, the fact that not only do they not belong here, but in my fucking housing spot and harassing us. The MPs surrounded them, and I was told minutes later to come to the station that was on the same grounds and identify them and give a statement. I was so relieved it was going to be over, the harassment and the 'Fatal Attraction' without the rabbit behavior from her. I got to the station and waited for about a half an hour for someone to come and talk to me and give me an update. A plain clothed CID walked in and introduced himself. I will just call him Johnson, a dick. He asked me the story again and I told him from start to finish of all that happened in Frankfurt, the arson, harassment and now this. He then asked me with a tongue in cheek type of way, like we were golfing or drinking buddies, "I was banging this girl?". I asked him what the fuck was' he asking that for, and where are they? when can I identify and charge them?". He told me he let them go, and it was an open post, and they are allowed to travel where they wanted. In total disbelief, I told him, "They do not belong in Army housing areas of families with children if they are not assigned here, they do not belong in my fucking parking spot harassing my family, and they certainly do not get to escape a investigation of arson I fucking told you about on the phone." Johnson then told me Frankfurt had nothing, and that he didn't believe her anyway when she claimed to be my lover, and they didn't investigate adultery when she claimed an affair. He told her to report to her local CID in Darmstadt Germany where she lived. He then said she was not satisfied, so she then said to him, maybe it was forced. Johnson told me at that point he told her "Now you are just making shit up, go report that to your own office and get out." I told him it was a mistake letting them go, but he insisted there was nothing he could have done. He advised me to prepare for any call or follow up.

I went immediately to the CSM under the general and explained everything that had transpired, from start to finish just like I did to the CID agent. I told him this is outrageous and should not have been allowed to be set free with no repercussions on them. He told me maybe they got scared now and it will blow over and to just maintain doing my duties and he will make some calls or let me know if he hears anything. I went back to the apartment, and talked to Nereida and said I think it was a good scare and the CID told them to pretty much fuck off and complain elsewhere with BS. I joked with Nereida about how I wouldn't be surprised if next I am accused of Rape or some shit. Well, NO SHIT!

Three days after this incident in my living area, the CSM called me to his office and said he was waiting for a call back from CID Johnson. I stood a few feet from in front of his desk until the phone rang. The CSM let out a bunch of "aha, aha, aha," and then a "really?". Then the dagger blow came, his face changed to shock, while he asked Johnson, "That serious?" while he quickly looked up at me like it was the first-time meeting and getting a look over. A few more aha and ok flew back and forth and finally he hung up. I stood at parade rest and prepared for what he had learned. The CSM told me that I was being accused of

Rape and Adultery. Forced sex, and automatically adds the adultery because I was married. I told him of course this was insane, and I was going to fight it and the whole nine yards. He waved for me to calm down and said, "That's fine and all but…. Here is the thing, you cannot be the driver for the general or around him in any way while this investigation is going on." That "I was now Flagged from any favorable actions and privileges such as my assignment to the general, leave or travel anywhere else, promotions, and now assigned to the administration office." (Bitch boy duty is like a prisoner getting laundry duty in prison.) Guilty until proven innocent. Flagged in the USA. I went to the colonel down the hall to see if I could speak to the general and assure him that this was totally groundless and give him the background on it. The general heard me and said he cannot hear anything I had to say, and to let it play out, but he cannot get involved. I was due to go back to the states and pick a last duty station to finish my commitment, but now all that was delayed, and possibly gone from the equation if I was found guilty of anything. I contacted my family, and I am sure Nereida did hers. My father said he would be coming over with my 3rd oldest brother Daniel, who recently graduated Law School and was already working prestigious positions. Nereida's mom would join them to help with Michael and comfort during this ugly period of our lives.

Until they arrived from the states to help, I was just staying busy at the HQ office doing admin work, cleaning, setting up conference rooms for meetings but no gym or anything that looked like I was not taking all of it seriously. I saw a soldier washing the General's car and it looked like I was already replaced. I made calls to the CID office demanding that if there was nothing else besides an accusation, then I need to be cleared so I could go back to the states when the orders come in. Johnson was the type that would blow smoke up your ass, and say "Yeah Yeah" then throw your case under a stack of cold ones and say, "I will get to it." My father, brother, and Mother-in-Law 'Mercedes' arrived. We got all the welcoming and baby time with Michael out of the way, some good eating, and now it was time to get to work on my case. They heard my whole side, and felt we needed to get someone who was an expert in both German law and UCMJ (Uniformed Code of Military Justice) that may have more insight, an influential push on my status, as well as obtain any evidence that they claim to have in discovery. We met and retained an attorney named Court. (No pun intended) who settled in Germany and had his own practice. He worked closely with Military JAG and German law. My brother Dan had the same intelligent etiquette and spoke with the same 'At the end of the day' type of approach and demeanor. My younger brother Greg is the same way and both very good at what they do and always there for me when I need them to this day. As children, we called Dan, 'head', because of his head being so big physically and even made up a song about it like we did all siblings. Now it showed for the real reason, that it was obviously for his brains and talent stored up inside that melon. He looked like Bruce Willis, and was tough, but a quiet genius in disguise. I felt hopeless about it all and he assured me by saying "You think this is even close to being done? you think I will allow this to happen to you?" then gave me the confident look that all would be ok. That is one thing about my siblings. They are very generous, but never will give you anything freely without ensuring there is an understanding and change of behavior or path suggested if it was substantial, to help you in any way and make you understand reasons behind it. He introduced me to Mr. Court and gave my background and how it fit into how this female was familiar with me and who I was with teaching classes etc. After a few brief meetings of what would happen and what can be done in time, I went for a run with my father around our housing area. He told me that this wench was allowed to hand in a skirt, and a blouse that she said were from the night "It allegedly happened" but she claims she has worn the skirt twice and the blouse 3 times since then, without washing them or some shit like that. She also claimed and named a date a year prior when I was out in the field with my last unit. I finally was allowed to see the statement she made, but of course with all the blacked-out areas when you do a FOIA request. (Freedom of Information Act). The statement was totally coached. Knowing her language limits, there was no way she said all the cop talk and covered bases that was interrogation/interview 101. This CID Johnson or whoever, totally asked all the myriad rape victim questions and checked the boxes and wrote it for her to sign this perfect English language, cop terminology statement. I made all these points to the attorney, to the CID and anyone willing to listen to the point they were sick of it. What else I learned was that one or more of my last unit members who were interviewed, had a few derogatory things to say, like I was a bragger, and was around this female at work and most likely involved with her but not anything to prove an affair or worse. So, shut the fuck up then, backstabbing assholes. Most likely the Staff Sergeant who walked up on her when she came to my gate giving me the Martial Arts Gi top. I told my father that she also claimed to be in my apartment and described it, which was scary because I never let her anywhere besides the MWR for class. My father said bluntly, "Terrence, I don't believe you raped this girl, of course I don't, but if you in any way had anything romantic with her, tell me and it won't be a surprise later and make you look even more guilty if they have proof. Like your stuff on her." I stopped running and told him to "Hold up and listen once again." I told him, "I know it looks that way, and I know that tone you have just like when I was in high school. But... I am telling you right now dad, I did not even hold hands with this girl, never mind doing what she said I did." "This is all because I embarrassed her and told her pretty much to fuck off with all the rumors and people talking. I was nice about it but then my car got blown up, and now this bitch is allowed to travel down here and destroy my life, fuck this and anyone who thinks I ever wanted that cunt." I then finished by telling my father "Dad, the only way that bitch could have my semen on her clothes is if she wiped a shower or tub full of my stuff after jerking off while tickling my balls with the jet stream from the handheld wand. Got it?" There is your visual.

There were a lot of things I wanted to do, I was frustrated and wanted my life back. Maybe it's just in my head but wouldn't it be interesting if I did things like, take my family and find the address they left on the statement so I can show up in their parking space at their house and give a wise ass wave and smile before taking off, just to see the shock and fear in their eyes and cause them to fear for their child's well-being like they did us? Would it not be entertaining to use my talent of impersonations, and imitate my CSMs voice, using his habit of a certain repeated motivating slogan, to find out the status with the 'evidence' being delayed and a final answer in the case, for the general to know, and to push for answer when I call for it? I also think that maybe someone should point out the fact that certain statements and evidence were allowed to be handed in, that should never have been. Even after a certain CID admitted to hearing her say affair, not rape at first and was turned down by this agent until she 'upt the ante.' It would be a shame for JAG to get a call from a general's voice on the phone "Suggesting" an internal investigation. Wow, the mind is a powerful thing. Just think if all those things just happened back-to-back to the point that I got cleared, and they admitted no evidence was found to prove either charge. So, 'to my surprise of course,' The attorney notified us all that the case is over, the evidence was not showing anything, that the statement was found to be a rant of inconsistent times and dates and obviously coerced or influenced in its terminology, and that I would be cleared to go anywhere I wanted and can return to work. I wonder what made the wheels spin faster? hmmmm.

The General met with me when I requested to see him. He told me again how he could not get involved during it but glad it worked out. He asked me where I wanted to go to finish my service after all I have been through and seen and done for the Army MPs and for him. To not let this be my legacy or memory of what I accomplished or did during my time and all else go to waste or be damned. I told him I was from Rockland County NY, and lived a short distance from West Point, where he graduated from. I said I would like to make sergeant while there and do desk sergeant work or go back to the gates away from people for a while. He said, "Consider it done."

I was flagged in the US Army, but now cleared to head back to The United States.

To be continued......**Devine 'Kung Fu' Intervention Part 2 "Full Circle"** ..coming soon! with more stories of : challenges, sex, relationships, violence, hardships, great times and proud times, family, loss, and much more of what I hope you enjoyed reading in my journey.

It is ALL -Kung -Fu... Life, Death, Good times, Bad times, Heartache, Hard work, Love, Family, Triumphs, and Tribulation.

Note and dedication:

During my writing and research for this book, I learned of the death of 4-star General Montgomery Meigs July 6th, 2021. He was 76 years old. To no surprise he had led, done and accomplished so much since we parted ways. He was a true leader, mentor and example that all soldiers and civilians alike should emulate. I look up and say thank you for the opportunity you have given me and the privilege of knowing you.

ALL RIGHTS RESERVED

COPYRIGHT 2022

DEVINE 'KUNG FU' INTERVENTION IS THE SOLE CREATION AND INTELLECTUAL PROPERTY OF

TERRENCE M DEVINE

ANY UNAUTHORIZED USE, DISTRIBUTION, OR SALE OF THIS BOOK AND ITS CONTENT IS STRICTLY PROHIBITED

DEVINE 'KUNG FU' INTERVENTION

TERRENCE DEVINE

DEVINE 'KUNG FU' INTERVENTION

TERRENCE DEVINE

DEVINE 'KUNG FU' INTERVENTION

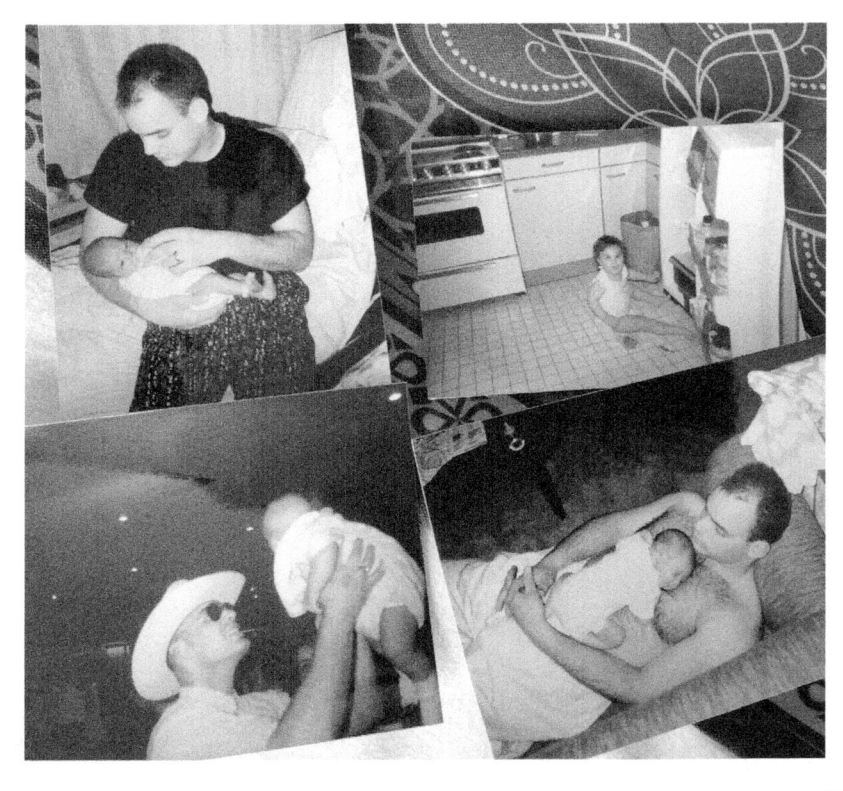

Made in the USA
Middletown, DE
19 March 2022